# MEXICO

## A HIGHER VISION

An aerial journey from past to present

ALTI PUBLISHING

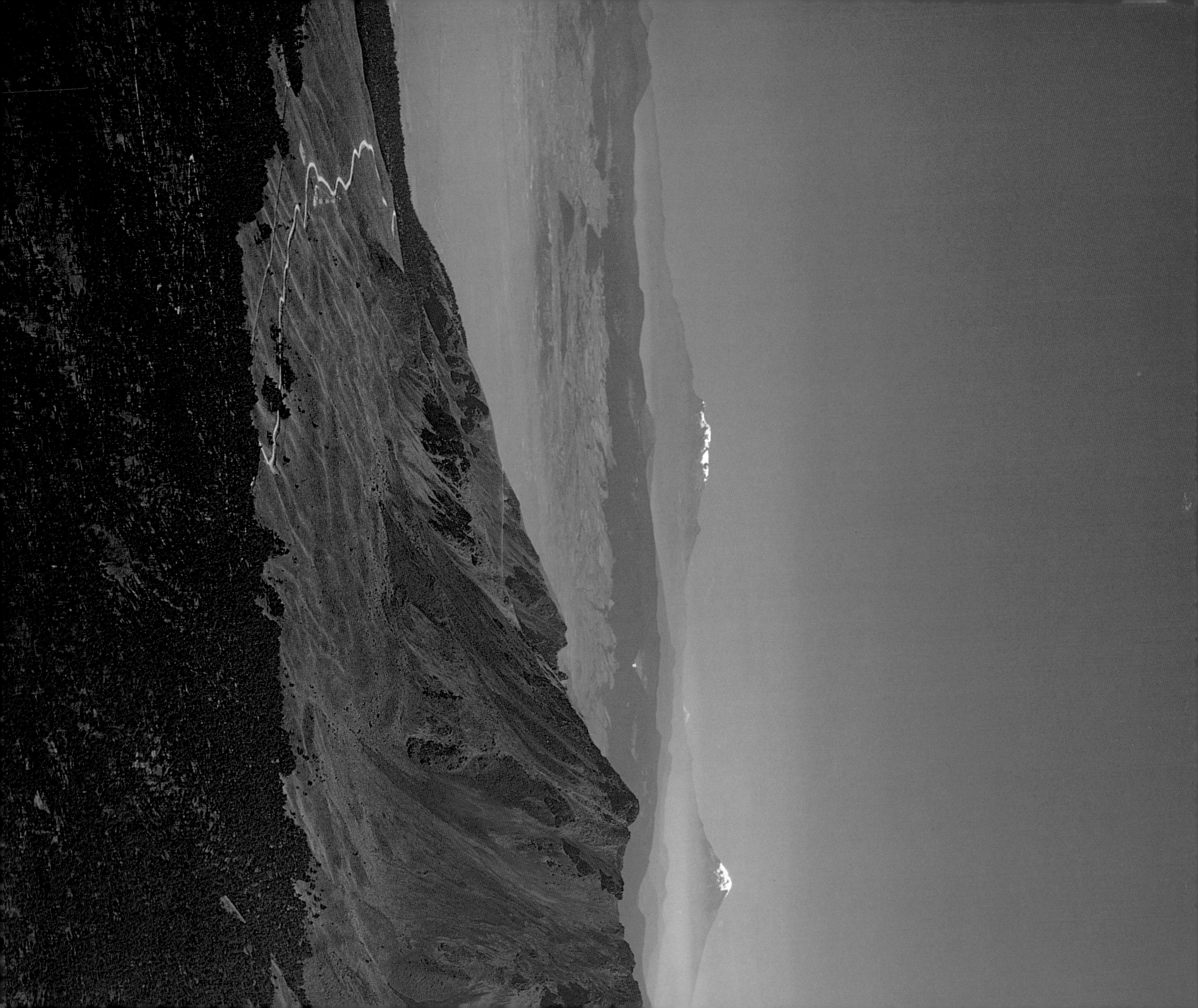

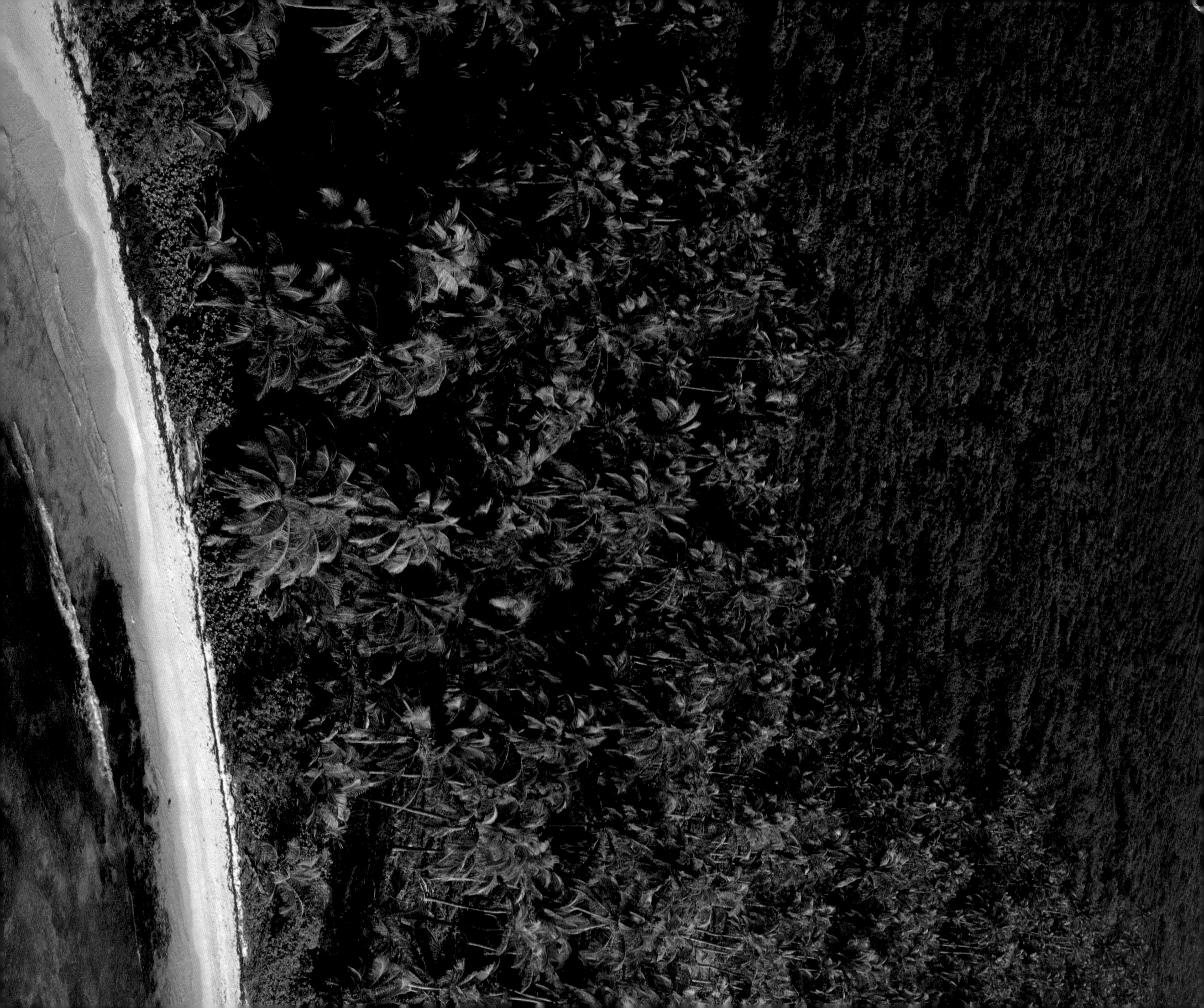

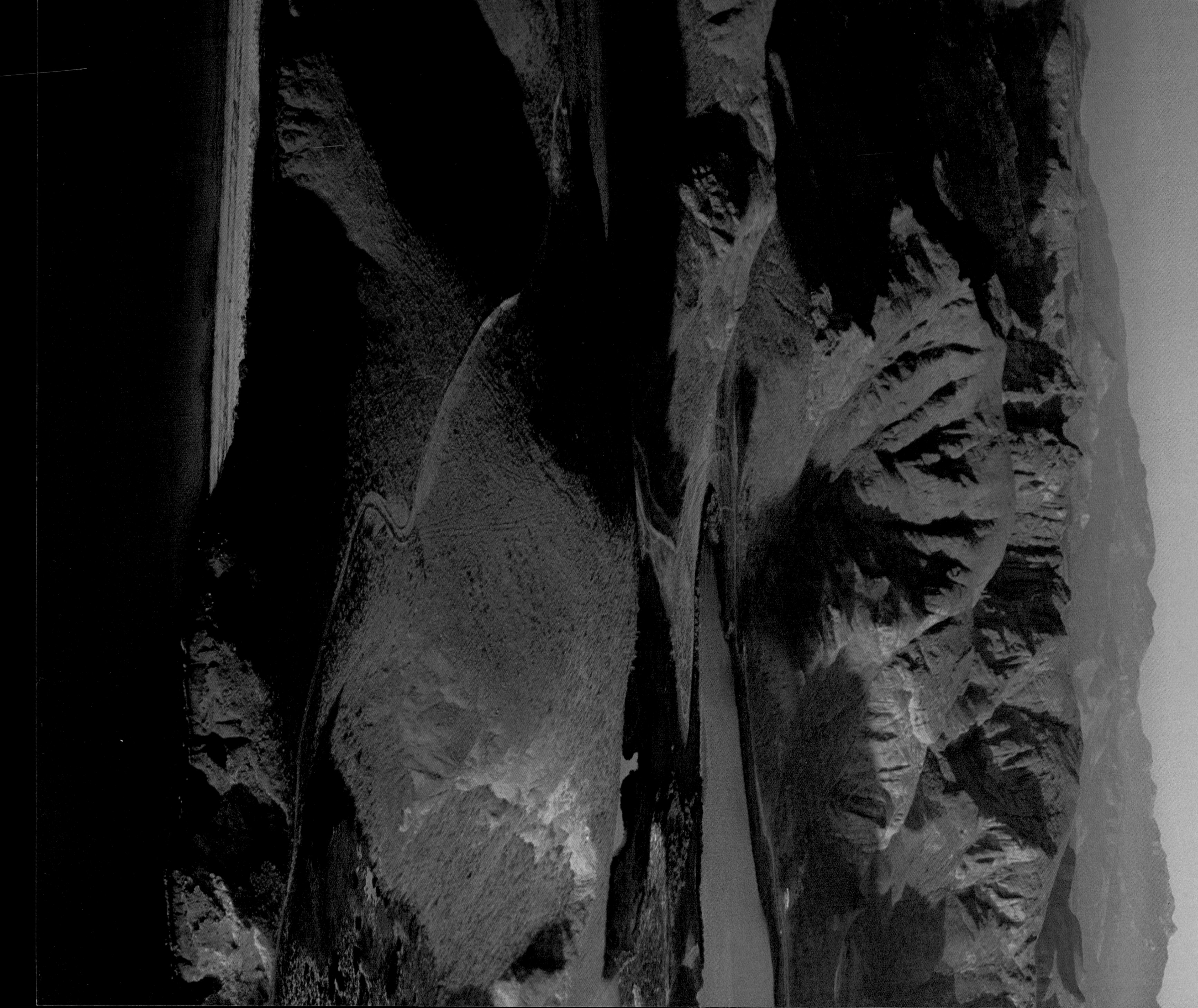

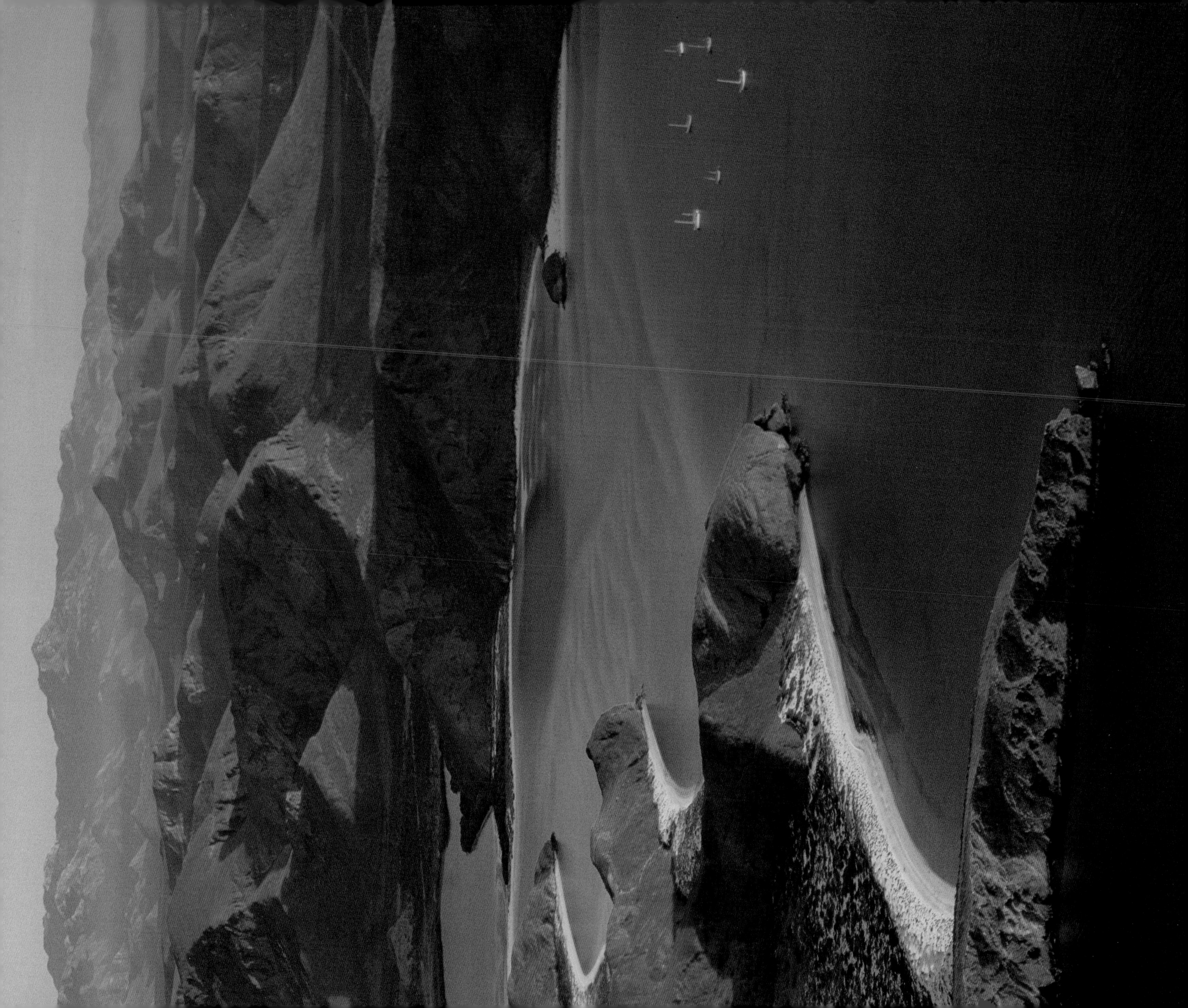

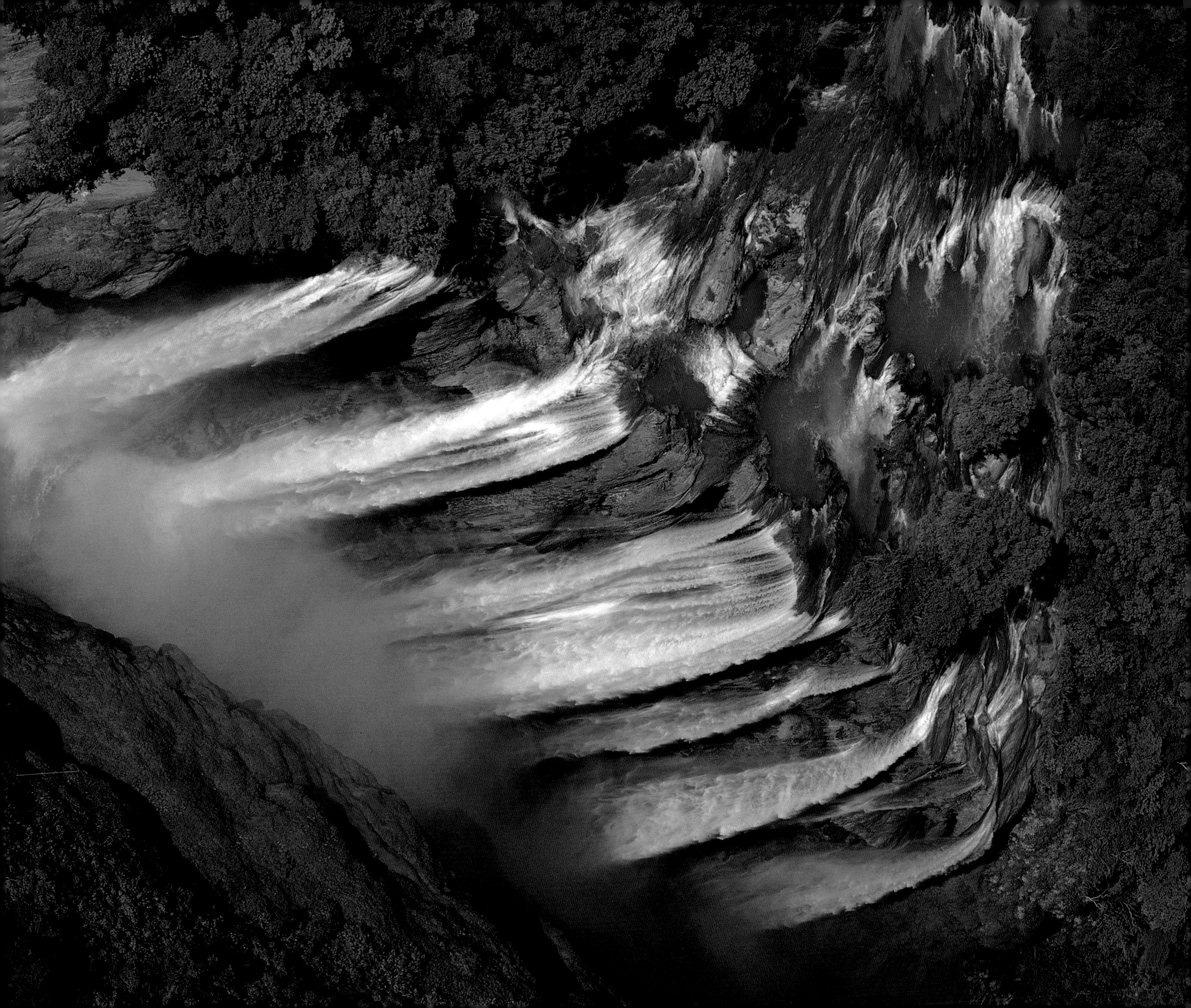

# MEXICO
## A HIGHER VISION
### An aerial journey from past to present


CARLOS FUENTES
Introduction

MICHAEL CALDERWOOD
Aerial Photography

MICHAEL CALDERWOOD
GABRIEL BREÑA
Text

# ACKNOWLEDGMENTS

**Aircraft pilot: José Manuel Muradas.**

We would like to thank the following for their help and hard work: Wayne B. Hilbig, Luis Fernández, Manuel Fernández, Robert Amram, Richard Lindley, the directors and staff of the Fundación Universo Veintiuno, Terry Sherf, María Kierkuc and Sandra O'Rourke.

We are particularly indebted to Manuel Arango, without whose wholehearted support and enthusiasm this book could never have taken off.



Alti Publishing
4180 La Jolla Village Drive Suite 520
La Jolla California 92037 USA

Produced by Martín Jon García-Urtiaga
Designed by Ana Elena Pérez
Introduction translated by Alfred J. Mac Adam

Published in the United States of America.

Library of Congress Catalogue Card number 89-081880.

ISBN 0-9625399-5-3

An edition of some of these photographs first appeared in 1987 under the title of "México visto desde las alturas", published by Fomento Cultural Banamex, Mexico.

**Third printing 1991**

Printed in Japan by Toppan Printing Company.

# CONTENTS

# PROLOGUE

## The face of creation

To see Mexico from the air is to look upon the face of creation. Our everyday, earthbound vision takes flight and is transformed into a vision of the elements. This book is a portrait of water and fire, of wind and earthquake, of the moon and the sun.

Not just one sun, but the five suns of ancient Mexican cosmogony. First comes the Sun of Water, which presides over the creation of the world and ends in the storms and floods that foretell the coming eras —Sun of Earth, Sun of Wind and Sun of Fire— each ending in catastrophe until we arrive at the fifth sun, our own, which awaits the final cataclysm.

This beautiful book confirms that ancient, aboriginal vision of the four elements succeeding one another in what was ultimately a circular movement. But the images of these photographs allow us to see beyond that spiraling circle to something even more beautiful: a circle, yes, and a spiral, but above all, a vision of the elements of creation in simultaneous interplay.

# SUN OF WATER

Coursing through these pages are serpentine rivers, mere threads of fertility in the midst of deserts, opulent tropical undulations pouring slow and wide into the sea. Over the flowing waters of the Papaloapan, river of butterflies, over the still waters of Lake Patzcuaro, furrowed by dragonflies, flutters the goddess Itzpapalotl, a star in the Aztec pantheon. Her very name, ''Obsidian Butterfly,'' resounds with the ambiguity of all the elements, her fragile multicolored wing at once a fearful sacrificial knife.

She is the first sign of creation, proclaimed by the fleeting, liquid element. It is not the nature of water to be always placid, and when it lies as calm as a mirror locked in the crater of a volcano, its image is ominous indeed, for its supernatural tranquility promises an imminent commotion. What are our years when seen against the mountains' millennia of stone? Who can really believe that these rock-encircled lakes in the craters of Toluca and Puebla always wore, and always will, this same metallic, motionless sheen?

Now everything moves again. The Usumacinta River flows on, inseparable from the forest it waters, equally inseparable from the clouds that gather over both jungle and river, as if they too were drawn along by the current. We know that all three —sky, river and jungle— hide and protect the civilizations that slumber beneath them, pretending to be dead, giving signs of life only in the mystery of the figures drawn on the rocks beside the Planchon River and in the ghostly processions of the frescoes at Bonampak.

The stillness of the waters is illusory. Majestic waterfalls cascade, washing away the land and its history. Mountains collapse into the sea. Sandbars break the very waters of the sea. And the surf on the coast of Jalisco shows the earth as a dark-clawed monster, besieged and battered by the fury of the sea.

The land is a portrait drawn by the sea. But we have only to turn the picture around to imagine the contrary. Is this not rather the portrait of the sea as it is attacked by a hungry, ferocious land, an ambitious, aggressive, imprisoned land that challenges the sea, ruler of the greater part of the planet's surface, for its dominions?

Unquiet, tremulous and insatiable, fearful and defensive, land of teeth and nails, jaws and talons—for a moment the land of Mexico shakes. The earth is about to speak. Earth will come to dominate water. The second sun comes to life amidst awe and terror.

## SUN OF EARTH

From the heights, the dead volcanoes —Popocatepetl, Iztaccihuatl, the Nevado de Toluca— signal that their silence is no insurance against catastrophe, but rather a portent of the next tremor. Paricutin, the youngest volcano, smiles like a mischievous child, warning us that one day a curl of smoke may appear in a Michoacan farmer's field, spiraling up from the bowels of the furrowed earth that shakes its shoulders, vomiting flame and ash until, in a matter of hours, it reaches the sky.

And there is more: Chichon, that dark, active giant, proclaims that its quaking and smoking will cease only in foreboding of the next great commotion of this restless land, where creation has not yet ended its labors. Each volcano ends only to pass the flaming baton to the next.

Sun of Water, Sun of Earth. From the air, we can see the origins of the land and all that flows over its surface. We can take a picture of the very point where the Sierra Madre Oriental begins, proudly abandoning plains and deserts as it starts its climb, then shoots toward its vibrant coupling with the western chain in the Nudo Mixteco. Linked forever, the two chains then run on together to their ultimate extinction at the southern extreme of the continent in Chile and Argentina, where the Andes bud off from the chain like frigid grapes. We can also take a picture of the source of the Conchos River and see the birth of its waters from the womb of the land.

In this book, we can now see all of this; which puts us there, present at the creation of nature. But not as something that happened in *illo tempore*, in the age of the gods, but something that is happening to us now, in our own time and under our very eyes.

The Nevado de Colima shows itself a mature gentleman, a bit gray around the temples, reminding us of the ambiguity of nature in Mexico. But neither he nor any of the great slumbering patriarchs watching over the earth can deny us our own time in this land.

For it is we —you and I— who see and touch and smell and taste and feel today, even as we witness the perpetual rebirth of the land here and now. We are the witnesses to creation, because of the mountains that watch us and in spite of their warning: "we will endure, you will not." Our response to this warning can be as sinful as pride, but also as virtuous as charity. We take the earth in our hands and recreate it in our own image.

Geometry, Einstein said, is not inherent in nature. Our mind imposes it on reality. In these photographs, man's geometric imagination is marvelously observed, from the air, in the incomparable clash of jungle and architecture in Palenque and Yaxchilan. It is at these sites that the primeval struggle between nature and civilization seems to have taken place; indeed it is still going on. Nature embraces architecture, but the human creation suffers because, while desiring to give itself up to nature's almost maternal tenderness, it also fears being suffocated by it. And, as human beings, we also fear that we will be expelled from that great, moist womb that nurtures and protects us and cast out into the shelterless world.

The great art of ancient Mexico is born from this tension between nature and civilization, between fear of enclosure and fear of exposure. The splendor of the great acropolis at Monte Alban and the sacred spaces of Teotihuacan are the triumph of but an instant of human domination, yet also human equilibrium, with nature. In these places, man has met time and made the shapes of time his own.

Nevertheless, man looks around him and sees the seductive threat of the sierras' deep gorges, the devouring tangle of the jungle and the latent tremor of the mountains. He responds by gently caressing the slopes of the mountains, festooning them with terraced gardens; by stroking the plains and planting them with wheat and maize; and by building cities, shelters of his own making to substitute for the protection of trees, caves and craters.

Mexico is a land of walls. Like all peoples, we built them first to defend ourselves against inclement weather, marauding animals and enemy attacks. Soon, however, architecture found other motives. First was the need to distinguish the sacred from the profane. Then came the need to segregate the conqueror from his subjects. And finally it becomes necessary to distance the rich from the poor.

In spite of these divisions, our cities, as these photographs demonstrate, transcend their own limits and, with the very walls that divide and separate, create movement, a circulation that re-unites us in the public square —the common place, the central site— and later in atriums and naves, chapels and portals, patios and gardens, until a network of communications is established which defies, and sometimes even defeats, the walls of isolation.

This is so because the human creation of the city acquires, in the Iberian New World, a sense of paradox. Civilization means living in the city, in the *civitas.* But in Iberoamerica the paradox is that the city is simultaneously a creation of the will and a product of chance. Perhaps this is true of all cities, simply because the *civitas*—the place of civilization, the space where we coexist—is also the *polis*—the place of politics, the space where we debate. And both civilization and politics, much as they may imagine themselves to be projections of the will, are also the result of both necessity and chance.

The cities of Mexico, I hasten to add, temper these characteristics with powerful admixtures of both tradition and novelty. First tradition: the energetic plan of the new Spanish city replaces its Indian counterpart, usurps its ceremonial, political and religious functions, only to find itself obliged to take them on anew. And then novelty: the Spanish American city offers the opportunity of creating new, regular, chessboard cities, as rectangular as the grid on which Saint Lawrence burned.

During the Renaissance, Leon Battista Alberti dreamt of making the ideal platonic city real. The novelty of America permitted this to happen. Here one can leave the walled agglomeration of the medieval city behind. But the past does not allow itself to be buried so easily. On the one hand, the previous tradition —the Indian center— struggles to reassert itself from under the very foundations of the new city, as recently happened in Mexico City when the Aztecs' Templo Mayor was uncovered in the central square, at the heart of the modern metropolis. On the other hand, racial novelty transforms both cities, the Indian and the European, into a mestizo city, a city of mixed bloods. And economic demands —mining, the haphazard topography of gold and silver— also cause the Renaissance city to revert to the medieval hive of narrow alleys, tunnels, stairways and pits.

From the air, Puebla, Oaxaca and Morelia display their checkered innovations, as well as their mestizo ambiguity, while Taxco, Zacatecas and Guanajuato yield to the serpentine cityscapes called for in the mining districts. Like the gold-seekers themselves, these cities scramble up the mountainsides, tumble down the slopes and sniff out their precious metals. When they find them, they adorn their altars with them, pave the streets with silver when their daughters get married, or lose their gold forever in a bet, on a whim, at a fiesta.

There is in this book a splendid photograph of the Barranca del Cobre, the Copper Gorge, in Chihuahua. Like the other canyons of the Americas, especially the most glorious of them all, the Grand Canyon, this great Mexican abyss bears witness to the two extremes of creation: birth and death. If this is a picture of the first day of creation, it is also a portrait of the last. The drama of these places does not end, nevertheless, in an affirmation of the beginning and end of the earth. Their greatest effect lies in the way such places define our frame of reference step by step as our vision moves through space. In Arizona or Chihuahua, the reality of these natural wonders is actually determined by our movements. A step to the right or left and the great stone abyss that we see changes so fundamentally that we never look on the same gorge twice. The movement of our body, our change in point of view, transforms what on the surface seemed an unalterable monument of nature.

Am I not defining the Baroque and searching for its specific American form? The Baroque is always an art of displacement, requiring the movement of the spectator if the work of art is to be seen at all—and, perhaps even more importantly, if it is to see itself. For the Baroque is a circular, not a frontal, art. The Byzantine icon can be seen from the front. Bernini and Michelangelo, on the other hand, invite the spectator to see the icon in the round. And when Velazquez, in Ortega y Gasset's phrase, liberates painting from sculpture in Las Meninas, his instrument of liberation is that circular gaze which enters the painting and observes the painter at work, as it were, from behind his back. In this way, the Baroque painting paints itself a second time.

But in Mexico, as throughout Spanish and Portuguese America, the Baroque goes well beyond the sensual intellectual reason of the Europeans. For among us, the Baroque is a necessity. It is a vital, resounding affirmation. Or better yet, it is the affirmation of a necessity. A devastated, conquered land, a land of hunger and of dreams, finds in the Baroque the art of those who, having nothing at all, want everything. The Iberoamerican Baroque is born of the abundance of need; it is an art desiring what is not there, a triple somersault over the abyss of desire with the hope of landing on one's feet on the other side and touching at last the object of desire: the fraternal hand, the body of love. The harsh, abysmal landscape of Mexico is, in its savage solitude, the picture of the Baroque need for its opposite: abundance and sharing.

The Sun of Earth, seemingly the most solid, the most long-lasting, thus shows that it too is a passing phenomenon. Its true image is that of a cloud in the artificial heaven of a Baroque altar. But the real heaven of Mexico offers more clouds than any altar. Clouds are the crowns of Mexico's second geography.

## SUN OF WIND

Ours is a country of prolonged, tranquil, luminous clouds. And clouds are the favorite daughters of the next sun, the Sun of Wind, that erodes coastlines and mountain peaks, that sculpts the stones and reshapes the tilled land.

At times, Mexico's opulent clouds are like a shroud tenderly shielding our eyes from a stiff or moribund body. In this book, clouds hide from us the agony of the Lacandon rain forest and its people. Both are fatally destined to extinction. At times, though, clouds are but the veil of civilizations unwilling to be disturbed. Most subtle of shields, the Sun of Wind protects all things in our country that await another time, a better time, to become manifest. In the meantime, clouds disguise the persistence of a sacred, magical world which the active, Faustian will of the West strives to annihilate.

Yet the clouds of Mexico carry out another, more disinterested task: they constantly soften the harder contours of the elements. Sea and land, volcano and air, ancient ruin and jungle, river and desert all clash head-on in Mexico. Here the elements war among themselves for their moment in the sun, and whole eras are named after each: water, fire, earth and wind.

Everything in Mexico vibrates simultaneously, perhaps because the clouds constantly soften the harshness of the imperious Mexican elements, so none truly triumphs over the others. Wind pushes the clouds, the airy spray dissolves the roughest peaks, clouds intertwine surf and shore and commingle waterfalls with cascades of flowers—hibiscus, bougainvillea, yellow marigolds for the dead. The cloud is an all-embracing mist, a smoke dissolving all things and rendering all distances deceptive.

An encounter and a coupling, at times a confusion, a triumph of light, a blurring of the slashing strokes so often present in Mexican art. The hardest lines of Rivera or Siqueiros are as fearful as the brutal natural encounters we see in this book. There is especially a photograph of the Isla Tiburon with its point —appropriately named Chueca, Crooked— like a shadowy wing menaced by a dagger-colored sea. It is as if the island wanted to fly away and the sea were holding it down, reminding the island that its destiny is to live between land and sea in perpetual confrontation.

The Sun of Wind then intervenes to dissolve all borders, to still every quarrel, to silence all shouts. In this sense, Michael Calderwood's photographic art in this book resembles the paintings of his compatriot J.M.W. Turner, the father of European impressionism. Among the best photos in this excellent collection are those of the Sun of Wind ruffling the sand, softly caressing the face of the water, revealing the texture of the undersea depths and pulverizing the many varieties of stone: porous, basalt, chalk and sand. In Mexico, this region of the air belongs to the painter Ricardo Martinez.

In this way, the Sun of Wind reveals a third Mexico within the very element from which we see the country in this book: the air. The wind that blows through the mouths of two twin gods, one Mediterranean and the other Mexican, Aeolus and Ehecatl, dissolves the rigidity of the earth and the immobility of the sea as they confront each other. The wind is a gift, a godly one. But like all divine offerings, it is ambiguous. And it has three names. The first is metamorphosis; the second is harmony. And the third is death.

The Sun of Wind transforms the unmoving landscape into a movable passageway. Things that seemed eternal prove to be changeable. Forms come together and pull apart to create new forms. The Pinacate crater in Sonora becomes a delectable woman's nipple. A river in Baja California acquires a surprising shape: a pink scorpion nestling in a bed of black earth. Are those real cows crossing the lagoon at Mexcaltitan, or merely a mirage? Aren't those fishing boats anchored around a buoy at Puerto Peñasco really a butterfly freshly emerged from the chrysalis of the sea? Are the cupolas of Cholula mushrooms? Are the tiger cages in Chapultepec Park made only of air?

Sun of Wind, my sun. On the cover of the geography book I used in school as a boy was a picture of Mexico as a horn of plenty, out of which flowed an overwhelming wealth of fruit as well as a long stalk of wheat that turned into the Baja California peninsula. That cornucopia appeared to be floating in mid-air. No hand, no land held Mexico up in the sky. It was like a free-floating planet of infinite riches.

I had to believe in the powers of the god of wind, Ehecatl, in order to hold in my imagination that Mexican cornucopia floating in the sky, scattering its fruits and fertilizing the fields with wind-borne seeds.

This volume reminds me of that old schoolbook. Looking through it is like penetrating the wealth of Mexico and discovering at one and the same time its permanence and its transience. For one moment, nothing changes and all the elements unite harmoniously. White birds resting in the waters of a power dam rob it of its engineered coldness. Cattle and wheat fields, derricks, hotels, haciendas, modern cities and beach resorts—these are all names for abundance. But do they express harmony as well? Perhaps real serenity is far more modest and intimate. I find it in an aerial view of Tlacotalpan with its peculiar knack for harmonizing gaiety and reserve. Here is a livable sensuality, the very definition of life in Veracruz.

Abundance also means the flight of the flamingos coming to feed, the pink blur of the birds on an orange sea, the silhouette of the jungles green shadows. The shock of Mexican colors and the mutable hues of nature come together in a recently repainted village church or in the haven of a Oaxaca hamlet. This is perfection, the harmony we long for, the peace of the elements.

## SUN OF FIRE

Peace does not last. The fourth sun, Fire, is ready to scorch the earth, to make it resemble those craters that —only because whimsy is more necessary than need itself— allow themselves the luxury of surrounding a cornfield near the sky. From the air we can see a soccer field, its outlines burned into the asphalt of the city like the burning graphics of that portrait of the sky on the earth at Nazca, in Peru, which can only be seen from the air.

There is a stony place in Chihuahua called Rocas de Lumbre, Rocks of Fire. Only the fire is not necessarily a visible flame but rather, at times, the paradox of burning water —the *atl tlachinolli* of the Nahuas— the inner conflagration we know, which knows itself, as death. As in the prose of the Mexican novelist, Juan Rulfo, the lowest-lying field and the highest mountain have a hole in them through which escapes the heat of death and sexuality. Eros and Thanatos, as we know, are both entryways into the invisible underworld, the Mictlan of the ancient Mexicans, where we enter wearing masks. We need another face for death, a mask that makes us acceptable for the other life—a better face perhaps than the one we had when we lived on earth, when we were bathed by water and animated by wind.

To see the Temple of Inscriptions at Palenque from the air is to look upon death. This pyramid was erected by Lord Pacal, to first anticipate and then commemorate forever his own death. From above, the extensive fields of cempasuchil, the yellow flower of the Day of the Dead, are a sign of the service nature always provides for death. Flowers the color of fire associate death with an invisible fire disguised as life: the Sun of Fire that proclaims death does not exhaust itself in death, even though it brings it, as it were, to life. For life in Mexico foresees death; it knows that death is the origin of all things. The past, the ancestors, are the source of the present. Now the craters are lakes, they are cornfields; once they were craters filled with fire. Could they be that again? Of course—just as life will come back again, because death precedes it.

The Sun of Fire is not, then, an omen of inexorable destruction and catastrophe, but a link in a circle where fire consumes air only to become its opposite, and then earth and then air again before it burns and starts the cycle over.

## AGAIN, THE SUN OF WATER

From on high, the four suns are consecutive but also simultaneous. As our gaze descends to the earth, it assigns precise names and places to each of the suns of creation. The name of Water may be Acapulco or Careyes, Puerto Escondido, Mazatlan, Veracruz or Cancun. Three seas, the Pacific, the Caribbean and the Gulf of Mexico, surround our land with more than six thousand miles of coastline. And these seas, although they are ours, bring news from the outside world on every wave.

From the Gulf coast the god Quetzalcoatl journeyed to the Dawn, promising to return to see if the people had put his principles of peace and brotherhood into practice. To that same coast came the Spanish conquistadors on the day prophesied for Quetzalcoatl's return, thus appropriating to themselves an omen that was theirs only by chance: the gods have returned to settle accounts with us...

The Gulf of Mexico became from that day on the last cultural port of call of the Mediterranean in the Americas. Soldiers and monks, scribes and merchants, pirates and poets, invaders and exiles, brought with them and carried through Veracruz the news of two worlds: America and Europe, Gulf and Mediterranean. Final resting place of the waves of the Bosporous, the Cyclades,

Sicily and Andalusia, the Mare Nostrum of European antiquity comes to end in Tampico, Villahermosa and Campeche.

But the waters of Mexico also send back their waves through the Atlantic to the Mediterranean, and their message is the news that the New World so desired by Europe is yet to be discovered, is yet to be imagined. It harbors mankind's oldest myths, its most secret truths, its dreams of the creation of the world and of man amid violence, pain, hope and joy.

"Let the day break!," exclaims the Popol Vuh. "Let the dawn appear in the sky and on the earth. There will be neither glory nor grandeur until the human creature exists..."

In Mexico's second sea, the Caribbean, an invisible sentinel stands guard at Tulum, waiting for the impossible return of the god. Sun and sea meet here. The watch is sleepless and eternal. But no god will return, because the earth is demanding that its children rebuild it, that they themselves be the creators now.

Finally, on the Pacific coast, the waves tell of a world even more distant than Europe. Cathay, the Kingdom of the Middle Earth. Cipango, the Land of the Rising Sun. And our vaporous sisters in the shadows, the Philippines. These are the islands and kingdoms that send us, as colonial poet Bernardo de Balbuena says in his Grandeur of Mexico, "Japan its silks, the South Sea its treasure of rich pearls, China its mother-of-pearl," so that:

*In you are their grandeurs condensed,*
*For you supply them with gold and fine silver,*
*While they give you things more precious still.*

The Sun of Water does not enclose us. It opens us, puts us in communication, breaks down the barriers of isolation; it makes us circulate within and without. We receive, we give, exchange, prepare the passage of water to land, of land to air, of air to fire, of fire to water again.

What we see in this book is a portrait of the cycles of creation, a portrait of the skies and the succession of Mexico's suns over Mexico, the authority that the country and its people derive from a relationship with the elements that gives no quarter. This book allows us to assimilate the portrait of the Mexicans with the portrait of creation.

That is why human victories are greater in Mexico. No matter how harsh our reality may be, we do not deny any facet of creation, we do not deny any reality. We try, instead, to integrate all aspects of the cosmos into our art, our way of seeing, our sense of taste, our dreams, our music, our language.

From the roof of Mexico, one can better appreciate this way of being. We are like Calderwood's picture of that sculpture of a god by Rivera which can only be truly seen at a distance, from on high.

This is a portrait of a creation that never rests, because its work is not yet complete.

Carlos Fuentes
San Jeronimo, Mexico
December 1989

# THE SOUTHEAST

## Land of jade and turquoise

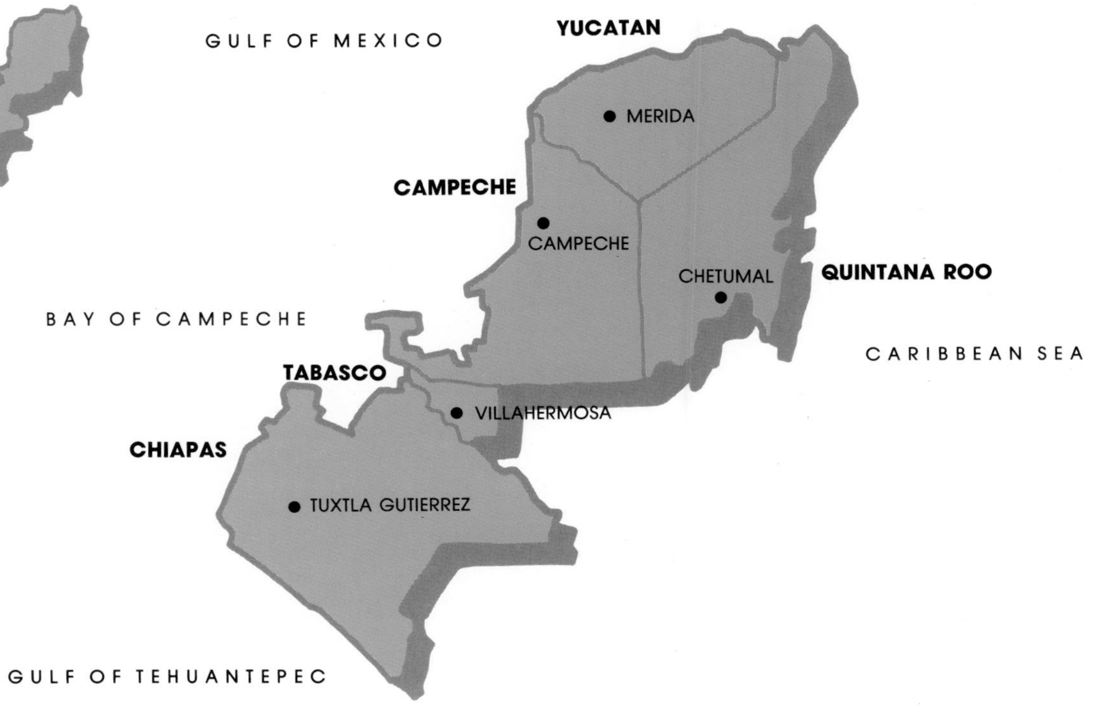


Until the days of paved roads and aircraft, Mexico was not so much a united country as a loose federation of regions virtually isolated from one another by a rugged geography. In some areas, the mountain ranges were so impenetrable that neighboring towns were practically ignorant of each other's existence. Today modern communication systems leap mountains and find remote villages, but unifying characteristics in so large and varied a country will never be easy to find.

Two widely differing geographies in southeastern Mexico, the Yucatan peninsula and the state of Chiapas, illustrate this diversity. A great limestone slab about a third of the size of France, the Yucatan can scarcely raise a hill to disturb the horizon. Because of very porous subsoil, rivers and streams are absent from the landscape. Since rainfall is the only real variable in the Yucatan geography, vegetation changes from abundant in the lower peninsula to sparse in the drier northwest corner. But the relative uniformity of the environment of the Yucatan is unique in Mexico.

Chiapas, on the other hand, presents a more complicated topography. The state is made up of a series of longitudinally defined subregions, each characterized by a different climate and ecosystem. The hottest area is the Pacific coastal plain, which serves as a corridor between Guatemala and Central Mexico. The adjacent band is dominated by a mountain range whose foothills are covered with coffee plantations. Beyond this mountain region lies the deep valley of the Chiapa River, where cattle graze on rolling grassland. Next comes a conifer-covered plateau. On the northeastern edge of the plateau, the land drops steeply into the tropical rain forest of the Gulf Coast, home of the Lacandon Indians, the last survivors of the jungle Maya. This strip stretches across the Usumacinta River into Guatemala.

Despite the geographic differences, Chiapas and the Yucatan do share a common bond: in these lands flourished the civilization of the Mayas, whose cultural influence was felt from Panama to central Mexico. Their ceremonial centers were masterpieces of pre-Columbian architecture and the hubs of a vast network of city-states that spanned all of southeast Mexico and much of Central America.

The Mayan civilization experienced two golden ages. The first, beginning around 350 A.D., resulted in the construction of a multitude of splendid cities, including Palenque, Edzna, Uxmal, and Chichen. This era of enlightenment, which was suddenly eclipsed after four cen-

The Agua Azul falls near the Mayan ruins of Palenque.

turies, was followed by a period of cultural hibernation. Then invading Toltec armies swept into the peninsula from the southwest, breathing new life into Mayan culture. The Toltecs built a metropolis on the site of the ancient city of Chichen, which they renamed Chichen-Itza. By the thirteenth century, this renaissance had faded, but was not completely extinguished until the Spanish invaded the Yucatan three hundred years later.

Although separated by the space of a century, the two golden ages of Mayan history have many common characteristics distinguishing them from other pre-Columbian civilizations. Mayan sculpture was far more ornate than the sculpture of other cultures of the time. Their cities conformed to no discernible model, although the overall effect is one always of harmony and balance. Their world was governed by a precise calendar, revealing the depth of their knowledge of astronomy and their obsession with time.

Their thorough recording of the movements of the heavens has helped archeologists date key events in Mayan history, but the reasons for the final collapse of their civilization have not been determined. Theories concerning the downfall include environmental catastrophe, internal power struggles, and barbarian invasion, but the tantalizing clues do not reveal the nemesis of the Maya.

Communications between the Southeast of Mexico and the rest of the country were maintained in pre-Columbian times despite primitive transportation technology. For much of the fifteenth century, Aztec envoys exacted tribute from communities in Chiapas and were only prevented from dominating the Yucatan by Mayan merchants. However, these trade links withered after the Spanish conquest of Mexico and Guatemala. To protect influential monopolies in Spain, the Crown obstructed trade within its dominions.

Cut off from the rest of the country by mountain ranges and unreliable roads as well as by politics, the people of the Southeast felt scant allegiance to a unified Mexico. The separatist movements that sprang up in both Chiapas and the Yucatan in the nineteenth century were the result of this isolation. During the Caste Wars, when the Mayan Indian peasants rebelled against ill-treatment by landowners, both sides were willing to compromise Mexican sovereignty over the region to win foreign support. The landowners explored the possibility of a colonial relationship to Great Britain, Spain, or the United States. The Indians at one point declared themselves the subjects of Queen Victoria. This allegiance not only failed to help the cause of the peasants, but served to further British interests by leading ultimately to the establishment of British Honduras.

The eventual pacification of the region contributed to a resurgence in the Yucatan's fortunes. By the late nineteenth century, Merida, the principal city of the Yucatan, enjoyed better public services than any other Mexican city. This new prosperity was founded exclusively on the exploitation of sisal, a fiber extracted from a species of agave known as henequen. As it grows in almost waterless conditions, the plant is ideally suited to the arid climate of the northern Yucatan.

By the second half of the nineteenth century, Yucatan landowners had established a world monopoly in sisal, supported by a system of immense plantations. Most of the fiber was shipped to the United States, where it was woven into rope and sacking. Lacking the flexibility to adapt once their monopoly was broken, the Yucatan producers became vulnerable to competition from Africa in the early 1920s. The development of synthetic fibers after World War II dealt the final blow to the sisal business.

To see any distance across the Yucatan, one must climb a pyramid or charter an airplane. Even then, the view is not especially engaging; a gray-green expanse of scrubby trees stretches in every direction to a level horizon. It is only near the coastline that the view becomes more rewarding; there the profile of the land is etched out in the brilliant blues and greens of the Caribbean.

Today the uniform landscape of the Yucatan is accompanied by very little evidence of its rich cultural history; a flash of white at a distance may signal the presence of a Mayan pyramid or the ruins of a henequen hacienda. A more familiar sight identifying this area are the towers of Cancun, cheerfully interrupting the dispiriting flatness of the coast.

The future of the Yucatan is now bound up in the fortunes of tourism. Thus far, Cancun has run ahead of all expectations. The flurry of development along the Mexican Caribbean and the increasing numbers of tourists who wander through Uxmal, Chichen-Itza, or Tulum are likely to provide the Mayan descendants of the Yucatan a new source of wealth. But for the Maya and other Indians in the highlands and jungles of Chiapas, who have maintained their traditional customs and social structure, a different path to a modern future will have to be found.



High-rise hotels in the resort city of Cancun cast their shadows over the Caribbean.

Palenque, a jewel of Classic Mayan architecture.

Pine and oak woods encircle the lakes of Montebello, Chiapas.

calm as a mirror locked in the crater of a volcano, its image is ominous indeed, for its supernatural tranquility promises an imminent commotion. What are our years when seen against the mountains' millennia of stone? Who can really believe that these rock-encircled lakes in the craters of Toluca and Puebla always wore, and always will, this same metallic, motionless sheen?

Now everything moves again. The Usumacinta River flows on, inseparable from the forest it waters, equally inseparable from the clouds that gather over both jungle and river, as if they too were drawn along by the current. We know that all three —sky, river and jungle— hide and protect the civilizations that slumber beneath them, pretending to be dead, giving signs of life only in the mystery of the figures drawn on the rocks beside the Planchon River and in the ghostly processions of the frescoes at Bonampak.

The stillness of the waters is illusory. Majestic waterfalls cascade, washing away the land and its history. Mountains collapse into the sea. Sandbars break the very waters of the sea. And the surf on the coast of Jalisco shows the earth as a dark-clawed monster, besieged and battered by the fury of the sea.

The land is a portrait drawn by the sea. But we have only to turn the picture around to imagine the contrary. Is this not rather the portrait of the sea as it is attacked by a hungry, ferocious land, an ambitious, aggressive, imprisoned land that challenges the sea, ruler of the greater part of the planet's surface, for its dominions?

Unquiet, tremulous and insatiable, fearful and defensive, land of teeth and nails, jaws and talons—for a moment the land of Mexico shakes. The earth is about to speak. Earth will come to dominate water. The second sun comes to life amidst awe and terror.

# SUN OF EARTH

From the heights, the dead volcanoes —Popocatepetl, Iztaccihuatl, the Nevado de Toluca— signal that their silence is no insurance against catastrophe, but rather a portent of the next tremor. Paricutin, the youngest volcano, smiles like a mischievous child, warning us that one day a curl of smoke may appear in a Michoacan farmer's field, spiraling up from the bowels of the furrowed earth that shakes its shoulders, vomiting flame and ash until, in a matter of hours, it reaches the sky.

And there is more: Chichon, that dark, active giant, proclaims that its quaking and smoking will cease only in foreboding of the next great commotion of this restless land, where creation has not yet ended its labors. Each volcano ends only to pass the flaming baton to the next.

Sun of Water, Sun of Earth. From the air, we can see the origins of the land and all that flows over its surface. We can take a picture of the very point where the Sierra Madre Oriental begins, proudly abandoning plains and

# PROLOGUE

## The face of creation

To see Mexico from the air is to look upon the face of creation. Our everyday, earthbound vision takes flight and is transformed into a vision of the elements. This book is a portrait of water and fire, of wind and earthquake, of the moon and the sun.

Not just one sun, but the five suns of ancient Mexican cosmogony. First comes the Sun of Water, which presides over the creation of the world and ends in the storms and floods that foretell the coming eras —Sun of Earth, Sun of Wind and Sun of Fire— each ending in catastrophe until we arrive at the fifth sun, our own, which awaits the final cataclysm.

This beautiful book confirms that ancient, aboriginal vision of the four elements succeeding one another in what was ultimately a circular movement. But the images of these photographs allow us to see beyond that spiraling circle to something even more beautiful: a circle, yes, and a spiral, but above all, a vision of the elements of creation in simultaneous interplay.

# SUN OF WATER

Coursing through these pages are serpentine rivers, mere threads of fertility in the midst of deserts, opulent tropical undulations pouring slow and wide into the sea. Over the flowing waters of the Papaloapan, river of butterflies, over the still waters of Lake Patzcuaro, furrowed by dragonflies, flutters the goddess Itzpapalotl, a star in the Aztec pantheon. Her very name, "Obsidian Butterfly," resounds with the ambiguity of all the elements, her fragile multicolored wing at once a fearful sacrificial knife.

She is the first sign of creation, proclaimed by the fleeting, liquid element. It is not the nature of water to be always placid, and when it lies as

# CONTENTS

# ACKNOWLEDGMENTS

**Aircraft pilot: José Manuel Muradas.**

We would like to thank the following for their help and hard work: Wayne B. Hilbig, Luis Fernández, Manuel Fernández, Robert Amram, Richard Lindley, the directors and staff of the Fundación Universo Veintiuno, Terry Sherf, María Kierkuc and Sandra O'Rourke.

We are particularly indebted to Manuel Arango, without whose wholehearted support and enthusiasm this book could never have taken off.



Alti Publishing
4180 La Jolla Village Drive Suite 520
La Jolla California 92037 USA

Produced by Martín Jon García-Urtiaga
Designed by Ana Elena Pérez
Introduction translated by Alfred J. Mac Adam

Published in the United States of America.

Library of Congress Catalogue Card number 89-081880.

ISBN 0-9625399-5-3

An edition of some of these photographs first appeared in 1987 under the title of "México visto desde las alturas", published by Fomento Cultural Banamex, Mexico.

**Third printing 1991**

Printed in Japan by Toppan Printing Company.

# MEXICO
## A HIGHER VISION
### An aerial journey from past to present


CARLOS FUENTES
Introduction

MICHAEL CALDERWOOD
Aerial Photography

MICHAEL CALDERWOOD
GABRIEL BREÑA
Text

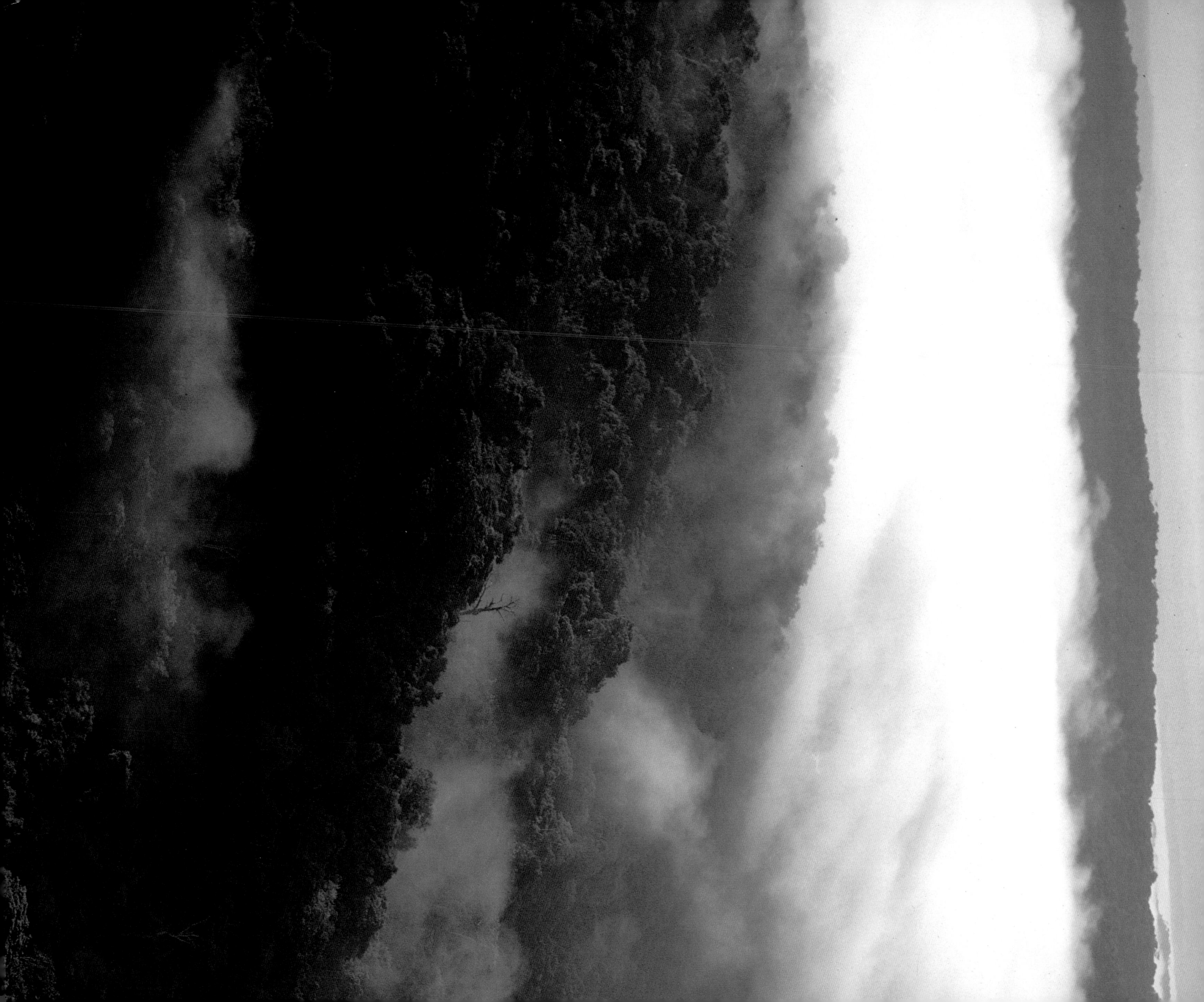

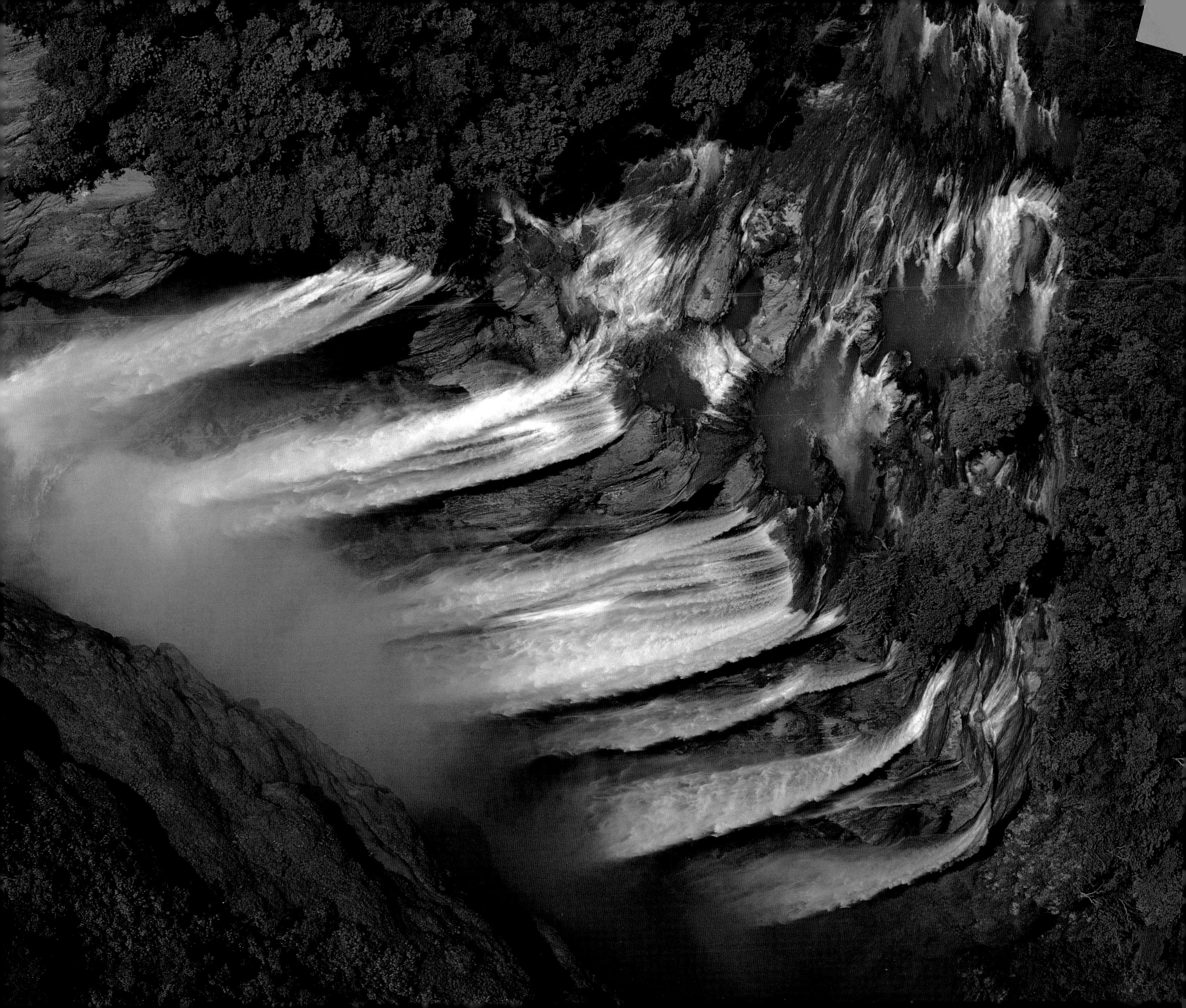

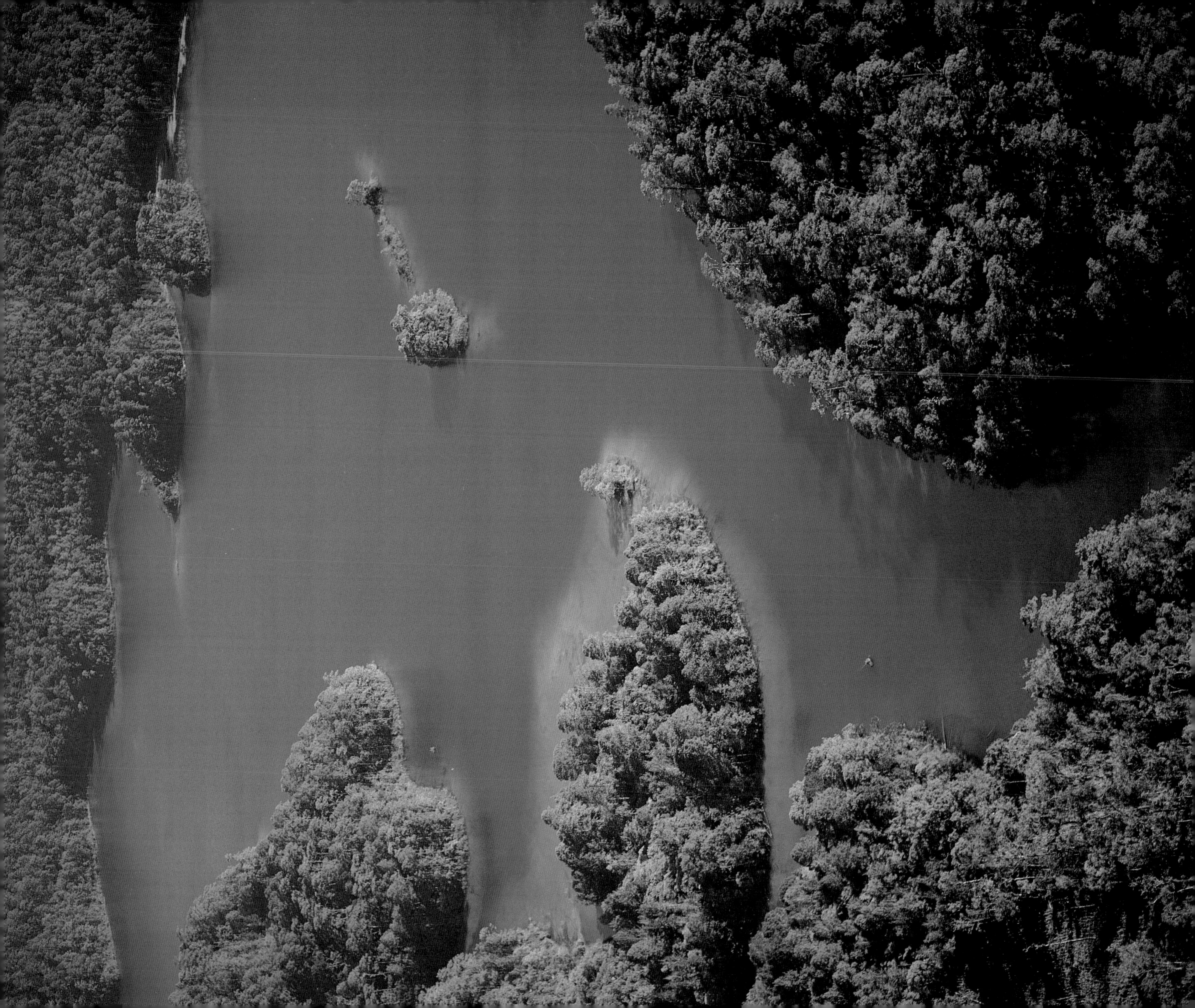

A fishing camp on the Gulf side of the Yucatan Peninsula.

A flamingo colony feeds in the shallow lagoon of the Celestun reserve.

The solitary ruins of Edzna, Campeche.

Ruins of an early Franciscan church, Campeche.

Mountain ranges in the highlands of Chiapas. ▶

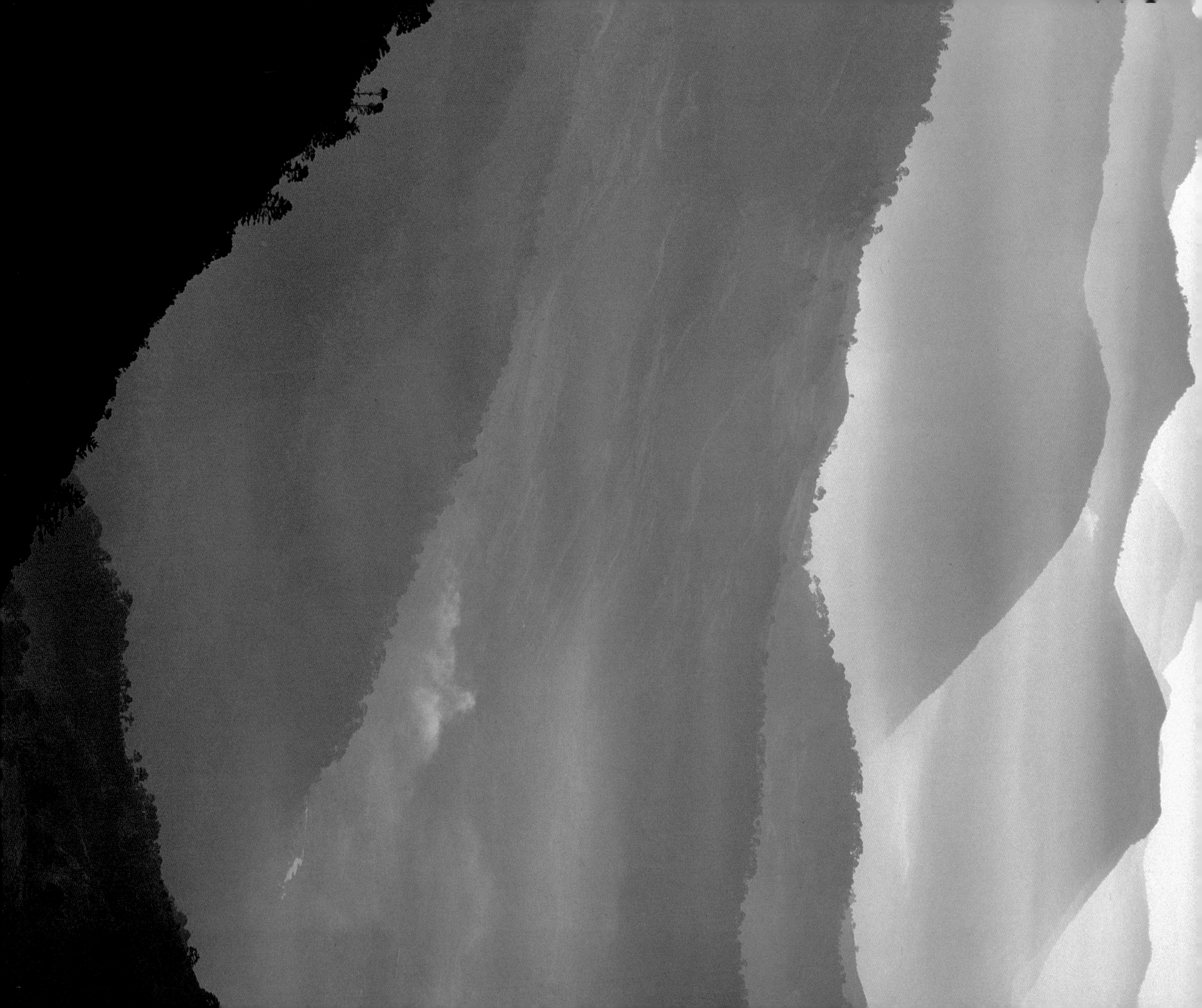

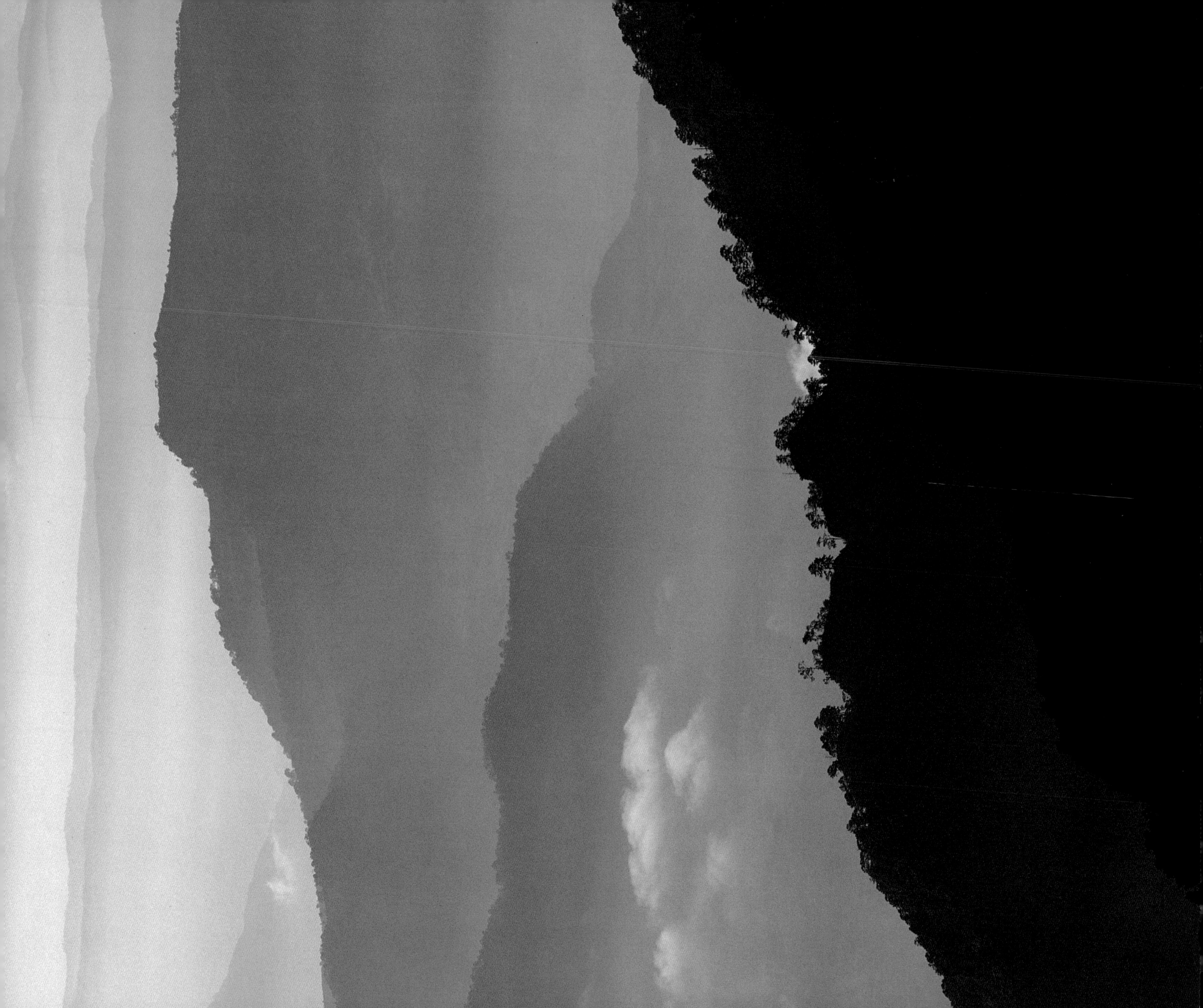

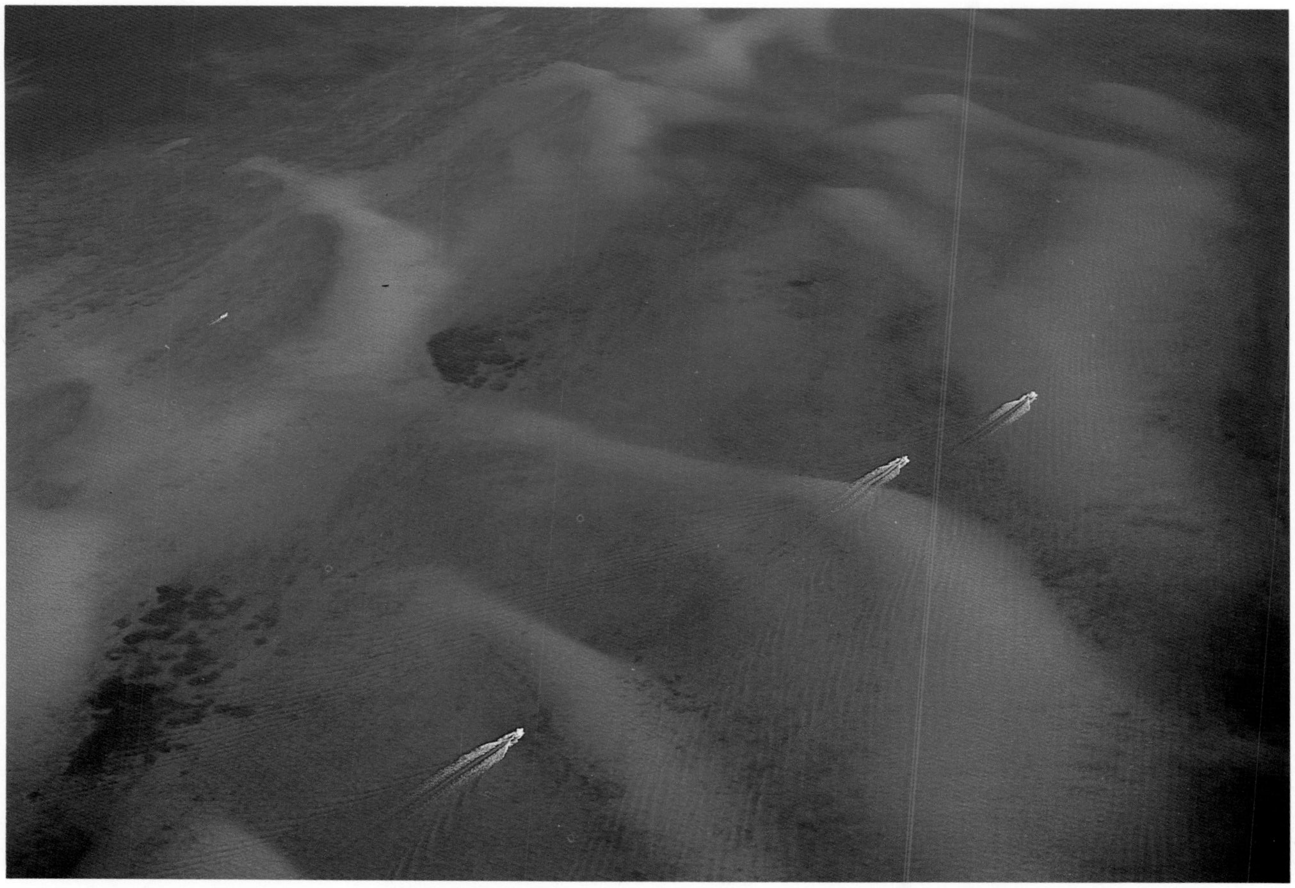

Shoal patterns in the Laguna de Terminos, Campeche.
Fishing launches cross the sandbanks off Isla Mujeres.

Early morning mist blankets the remnants of the Lacandon jungle.

The fissured slopes of El Chichonal, a newly active volcano in Chiapas.

El Castillo, the pyramid dedicated to the serpent god Kukulcan at Chichen-Itza.

The temples of Yaxchilan emerge from the Lacandon rain forest.

The hacienda of Blancaflor, Yucatan.

Evening thunderstorm bearing down on Isla del Carmen, Campeche.

The Tzotzil Indian town of San Andres Larrainzar, Chiapas.

The great Mayan ceremonial center of Uxmal.▶

# THE GULF COAST

## The flow of time

In the spring of 1519, when the first Spaniards led by Hernan Cortes stepped ashore on the sultry beaches of Mexico's Gulf Coast, they were confounded by the sight of a white-capped volcano shimmering above the haze to the west. "The natives tell us it is snow," wrote Cortes to his king, "but the place is so hot that we cannot affirm that it is indeed snow, since we have not seen it for ourselves, even though we have been very close." Months later, on their march from the lowlands to the great capital of the Aztecs, Cortes sent a group of men to climb another volcano and wrote afterwards: "They brought abundant snow and icicles for us to see, because it seemed so strange, being, as we are, where there is continually so much heat, at 20 degrees, on the same parallel as the Isle of Hispaniola."

To reach the highlands of the Sierra Madre Oriental, Mexico's great eastern mountain range, the Spaniards followed essentially the same route a modern traveler must take when driving up from the city of Veracruz. From the air the terrain resembles a giant staircase, but only the lowest step —the plain separating the sea from the mountains— is apparent to the land traveler. The subsequent steps are disguised by ravines, cliffs, and hidden valleys. Although the topography is obscured by the terrain of the Sierra, a sequence of cooler climates is clearly recognizable, and the changes in vegetation remind the traveler of his gradual ascent from the coastal plain. The Spaniards named the regions somewhat arbitrarily according to temperature: *tierra caliente* for the hotter low-lying plains and foothills, and *tierra fria* for the cooler plateau starting about a mile above sea level.

Although it shares the latitudes of the barren Sahara, the Gulf Coast of Mexico is a geography of lush plant growth. Two climatic factors resulting from intense solar radiation —evaporation and wind— combine with the geographical juxtaposition of the sea alongside the Sierra Madre to create a moist climate. Because sea water evaporates readily in the heat, the atmosphere is saturated with humidity and cloud formation is abundant. Tropical winds carry clouds toward the mountains where they condense and release rain. The same process, incidentally, occurs on the Pacific Coast, but on the Gulf it is augmented by the prevailing winds blowing out of the east. Rain falls so plentifully on the slopes of the Eastern Sierra Madre that the Gulf watershed accounts for more than half of all surface water resources in Mexico.

The San Pedro y San Pablo River winds across the plain of Tabasco.

Because of these climatic factors the *tierra caliente* of the Eastern Sierra Madre is alternately sluiced with rain and warmed by tropical sunshine, a phenomenon that has led to the creation of an incomparable botanical garden. Biologists calculate that as many as ten thousand species of plants grow in the area, and an abundance of exotic animals inhabit this paradise. Orchids hang from the branches of zapote trees and the cries of cockatoos and parrots fill the air.

The climate is also beneficial for farming. The first European settlers planted sugar cane in the valleys. They later harvested vanilla, which was greatly prized in the eighteenth century for flavoring chocolate. Today the mountain slopes are covered with coffee plantations, interspersed with orchards of papaya, banana, avocado, grenadine, custard apple, mango, and citrus trees. Closer to the coastal plain, local species of wild yam are harvested as the raw material of steroids. Around the city of Jalapa, Holstein cows browse on lush meadows as if they had just stepped out of a Swiss calendar.

Over six hundred miles long, the Gulf massif tapers into the lowlands of the Isthmus of Tehuantepec. As the coastline bends around the Bay of Campeche, the mountains recede and the plains broaden. Water lies everywhere—in rivers flowing sluggishly to the Gulf, in swamps where unwary cattle disappear, and in ponds which overnight become lakes if the rivers overflow their banks. The local folk often find it easier to travel by boat than by road.

Some 3,500 years ago, from these same swamps and rain forests which lie today in the state of Tabasco, there emerged Mexico's seminal pre-Columbian civilization. The origins of the Olmec people are obscure, but archeological evidence indicates that their spiritual and aesthetic creativity influenced every Middle American culture of importance for the following 3,000 years. The Olmecs brought order to the terrifying randomness of natural phenomena through the invention of the calendar, which also provided the priestly elite with the knowledge that enabled it to control the greater mass of the population. As befits the climate, the jaguar god worshipped by the Olmecs was the precursor of the omnipotent rain deities. Olmec sculptors carved the hardest jade stones into delicate figurines and blocks of basalt into gigantic heads of remarkable symmetry and expression. By grouping their communities around ceremonial centers inhabited by religious hierarchies, the Olmecs set the basic pattern of pre-Columbian social organization. Through a system of tribute they mastered their less sophisticated neighbors and their merchants traded from Panama to the Mexican Pacific.

By an ironic twist of history, the Spaniards set out on their conquest of pre-Columbian civilization from the same shores which nurtured the Olmec mother culture. At the site of their landing the Spaniards founded the port of Veracruz. Meaning "the True Cross," the name embodies the spirit of righteousness by which Spain justified its conquests. Historically the gateway to Mexico, Veracruz has experienced the passage of friend and foe alike. In the colonial period, the fortress of San Juan de Ulua was built to protect the port from pirate raids. Later this fortress became the last Spanish stronghold in Mexico. It was finally surrendered to the Mexican navy four years after the treaties of independence from Spain had been signed. Even in the post-independence period, the port continued to be a center of conflict; as late as 1914 Veracruz drew the unwelcome attentions of foreign warships and invading armies.

At the turn of the century there flowed from the earth of the Gulf Coast a new source of wealth. The Aztecs called it *chapopotli* and chewed it to clean their teeth. Petroleum, as it is known today, was initially refined for use in lamps. By World War I, a forest of oil derricks had sprung up among the orange groves of Veracruz. When the oil industry was nationalized in 1936, Mexico ranked among the world's foremost producers. Advances in drilling techniques, coupled with rapid price increases in the 1970s, allowed Mexico to tap the enormous reserves below the Gulf sea bed. But long-term instability in the international oil market has shown that oil may play a cruelly ambivalent role in a nation's fortunes.

Generations of Mexicans have looked upon the Gulf region as a replica of the Garden of Eden. In tending the garden, the people of Mexico have fared little better than their Biblical predecessors. Centuries of misuse have exacted their price from the environment. Major waterways are badly contaminated and the thick woods of ceiba trees which once covered the mountain slopes have been reduced to a few threatened clumps. Pre-Columbian cultures living in this area revered nature and present-day Mexico would pay suitable homage to its ancestry if it could find the road back to environmental harmony. The Gulf Coast can only reclaim its reputation as a paradise on Earth by balancing the progress of human civilization with care and respect for natural resources.



The sun sets behind a petrochemical refinery at La Cangrejera, Veracruz.

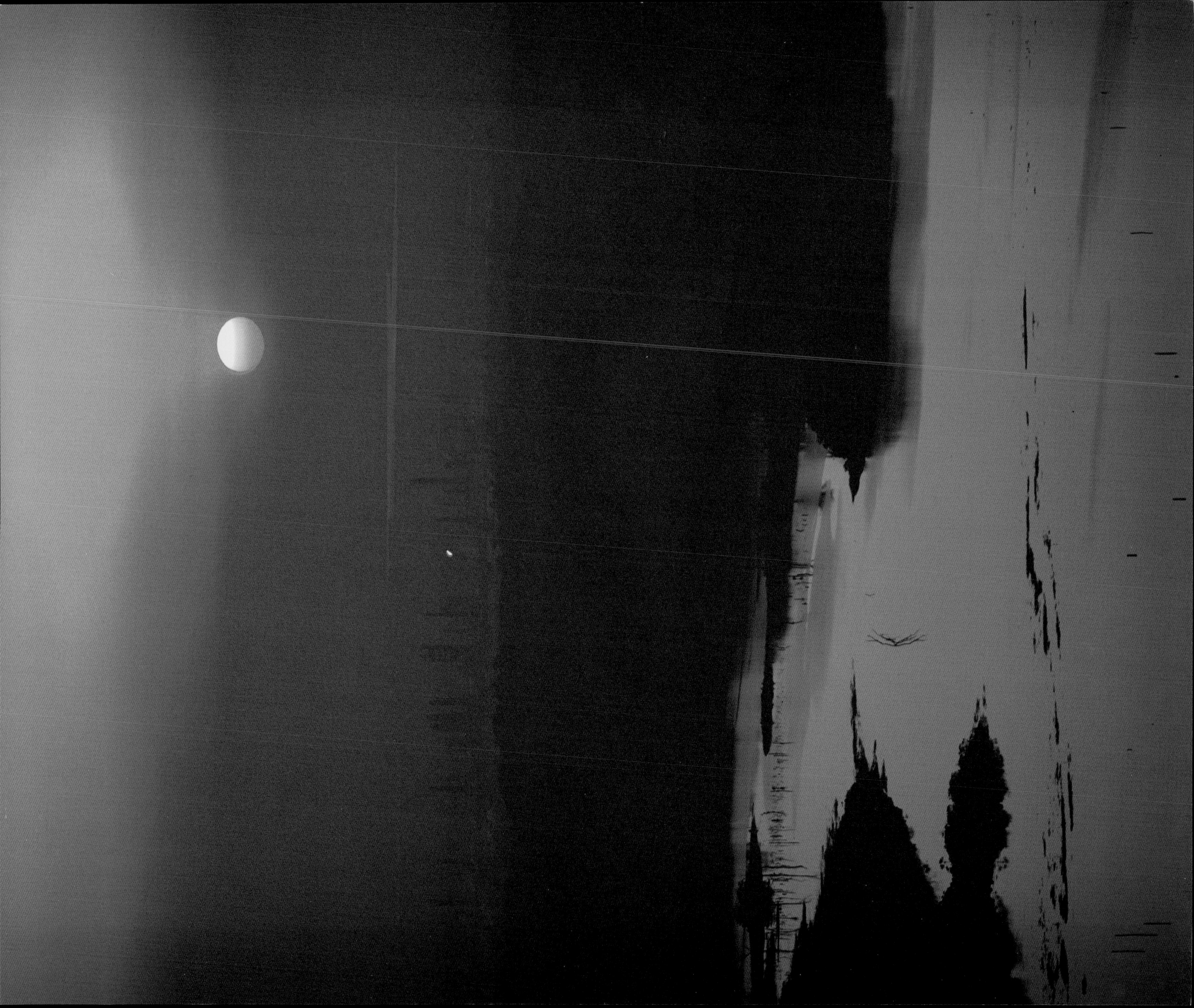

El Salto waterfall in the Huasteca region, San Luis Potosi.

Early morning clouds surround the cone of the Pico de Orizaba.▶

Primavera trees in full bloom on the coastal plain, Veracruz.

A Pemex oil rig 40 miles into the Sound of Campeche.
Veracruz, Mexico's oldest and busiest Gulf port.

Petroleum tanker moorings in the Coatzacoalcos River, Veracruz.

An example of Mexican native art, Cupilco, Tabasco.

Porticos and balustrades line the streets of Tlacotalpan, Veracruz.

The foothills of the Tuxtla volcanos by Playa Escondida, Veracruz.



The Miguel Aleman Reservoir in the State of Oaxaca.

# THE CENTRAL PLATEAU

A cultural magnet

The city of Puebla, sixty miles southeast of Mexico City, lies closer to the Equator than Cairo, Mecca, or New Dehli, yet summers are cooler than in most of the United States. Despite the altitude of 6,500 feet above sea level, winter months are rarely harsh. Puebla is typical of the climate extending through Mexico's central plateau which comprises much of the states of Queretaro, Morelos, Puebla, Mexico, Michoacan, Jalisco, Guanajuato, Hidalgo, and Tlaxcala. The Mexican plateau is not a flatland like the Midwest of the U.S. It is more like a maze of fertile valleys weaving crooked paths between the mountain ranges.

At both its eastern and western edges, the plateau fractures into a multitude of ravines. The northern limit is marked simply by a gradual change of climate from temperate to arid at the latitude of the city of Aguascalientes. But to the south a formidable wall of volcanos, including the five highest peaks in Mexico, bisects the country from ocean to ocean, dramatically separating the plateau from the lower Pacific Coast area. Volcanos have continued to erupt along this chain for more than forty million years.

Barely fifty years ago, a farmer in Michoacan noticed smoke rising from the furrows of a newly plowed field. Eight months later the field, the surrounding woods, and the farmer's village of Parangaricutiro lay buried beneath the lava that flowed from a cinder cone rearing 1,500 feet into the sky. The fires of Paricutin eventually subsided, although they still simmer beneath the surface; but other volcanos in the area, notably the Volcan de Fuego, are active and occasionally shake the earth around them.

In area, the plateau is larger than West Germany and home to more than half the population of Mexico. It is also the cradle of Mexican politics, the studio of the arts, and the hearth of Mexican cuisine. Two great achievements of human civilization were initiated for the American continent on the central plateau of Mexico: the domestication of corn which promoted settlement into agriculturally based communities and the subsequent establishment of major urban societies.

Archeological evidence suggests that hunters roamed the central plateau as early as 24,000 years ago. Then, around 1,000 BC, the hunters discovered how corn, originally a wild steppe plant, could be cultivated as a reliable source of food. The cultivation techniques developed by these early farmers were extended later to beans, squash and chiles.

Corn is the best example of the interaction between human farmers and their food sources. Although corn is a hardy crop and can be grown in most climates, the seed grains must be stripped from the husk and scattered if the

The Paricutin cinder cone, recent proof of Mexico's volcanic geography.

number of plants in a stand is to multiply. Because of this relationship, corn was transformed from a scattered grass with tiny kernels to an extensively cultivated grain providing a major staple food for the world and a widely used raw material for a multitude of food products.

An example of a major urban community established on the central plateau of Mexico is Teotihuacan whose remains are to be found thirty miles northeast of Mexico City. Of the hundreds of archeological sites strewn across the central plateau, none is more imposing or enigmatic than Teotihuacan. Around 700 A.D. the city-state apparently supported a population in excess of a hundred thousand. European cities would not reach comparable proportions until the Renaissance nearly 800 years later. Long after it had been abandoned, the city commanded the respect of every civilization that later controlled the central plateau. Teotihuacan is an Aztec name meaning "home of the gods."

The people of Teotihuacan had only stones for tools and human labor as a source of power. The production of food depended on a variable rainy season, allowing perhaps for the survival of scattered villages, but not for a densely populated city. Still, the economy of Teotihuacan supported not only the peasants who farmed the land, but also the upper classes of craftsmen and priests. Modern civilization, seeing itself as the pinnacle of human achievement, finds the scale and social diversity of this ancient metropolis difficult to comprehend. To resolve the enigma of Teotihuacan, skeptics have resorted to fantastic theories of extraterrestrials who bestowed their cosmic wisdom upon unenlightened but adoring savages. However, the cultural era of Teotihuacan spanned almost a thousand years; certainly a sufficient time to develop a large population and a culturally sophisticated society.

Owing to more favorable weather conditions, most pre-Columbian societies were concentrated within the southern half of the central plateau, around the lagoons of Patzcuaro and Texcoco, and in the Valley of Puebla. However, the Spaniards, lured by the promise of gold and silver, settled the northern half, especially the Lerma River basin. Once the mines were open, they were supplied by trading posts which grew, in the cases of Queretaro and San Miguel de Allende, into cities that rivaled the mining centers themselves in wealth and magnificence.

On the other hand, cities like Guadalajara and Morelia were laid out in farmland and prospered from agriculture and stock breeding. The poor quality of grassland in Mexico, where each head of cattle may need up to thirty-five acres of grazing area, obliged the drovers to improvise new herding techniques. Saddles were modified to accommodate long hours of riding, cow-punching skills were perfected, hat brims were broadened against the Mexican sun: the image of the *charro* was born.

The structure of colonial society was centered around the Catholic church, whose power transcended on occasion even that of the viceroy, the representative of the Spanish Crown in Mexico. Schools and hospitals were managed by the multiple religious orders, such as the wealthy and influential Company of Jesuits whose liberal philosophy was disseminated through their educational institutions.

The Jesuit college of Tepotzotlan was founded on the northwestern rim of the Valley of Mexico and endowed with great wealth. It was one of fifty-three similar institutions educating mainly the children of Mexican-born aristocrats. Pupils were taught to appreciate the value of their birthright, to take pride in the virtue of Mexican customs, and to extol the Mexican landscape. The Jesuits even ventured to study pre-Columbian societies, a practice which the Church considered almost heretical. Because they contributed greatly to a distinctive Mexican consciousness, their work found little favor in imperial Spain. The Jesuits were banished from the Spanish dominions in 1767, but echoes of their teaching could be heard fifty years later in the ideas inspiring the early leaders of the independence movement.

The great events ruling the destiny of Mexico have been played out, for the most part, on the stage of the central plateau. Whether in short, violent chapters such as the Spanish Conquest and the War of Independence, or in developments such as the domestication of corn and the emergence of nationalism, change has spread outward from the center of the country. It is tempting to find a comparison in Mexican geophysics, where earthquakes and volcanos rearrange the earth around them in outward-moving patterns. In time the topography of the plateau will be altered by the same natural forces that produced its present shape. However, human affairs are not so easily predicted. Only time will tell whether, in the quickening pace of contemporary events, the political and cultural magnet at the center of Mexican history will hold its power.



Early morning mist rises from a hillside near Apan, Hidalgo.

A crater provides a ready-made wall for a farmer's field.

Mexico's oldest bullring during the spring fair of San Marcos, Aguascalientes.

Agricultural terracing cut into the hills of the Sierra de Tentzo, Puebla.

Ripening wheat fields near Apan, Hidalgo.

Uneven terrain forced the abandonment of the traditional street grids in Taxco (left) and Guanajuato (right).

The Pyramids of the Moon (above) and the Sun (right), Teotihuacan.

Strip field patterns surround a Puebla village.
A bend in the Atoyac River, Puebla.

*Charro* traditions were founded in the stockraising ranches of Jalisco.

Erosion patterns in the highlands of Jalisco.

Fields of African marigolds destined for Day of the Dead graveyard altars.

The tower and nave of Parangaricutiro church jut from the Paricutin lava beds.

Church in Jolalpan, Puebla.

Water-filled craters of long extinct volcanos on the plains of Puebla. ▶

A unique arrangement of plazas surrounding the Cathedral of Guadalajara.

The domes and belltowers of Guadalajara silhouetted against the rising sun.

An irrigated plain dotted with *huizache* trees, Puebla.

The Hacienda of Chiautla, an architectural curiosity in Puebla.

Country church, Puebla.

The cupolas of the Royal Chapel in the monastery of San Gabriel, Cholula.

Lake Patzcuaro, former site of the Purepecha Indian civilization.

The main square of San Miguel de Allende, shaded by clipped laurel trees.

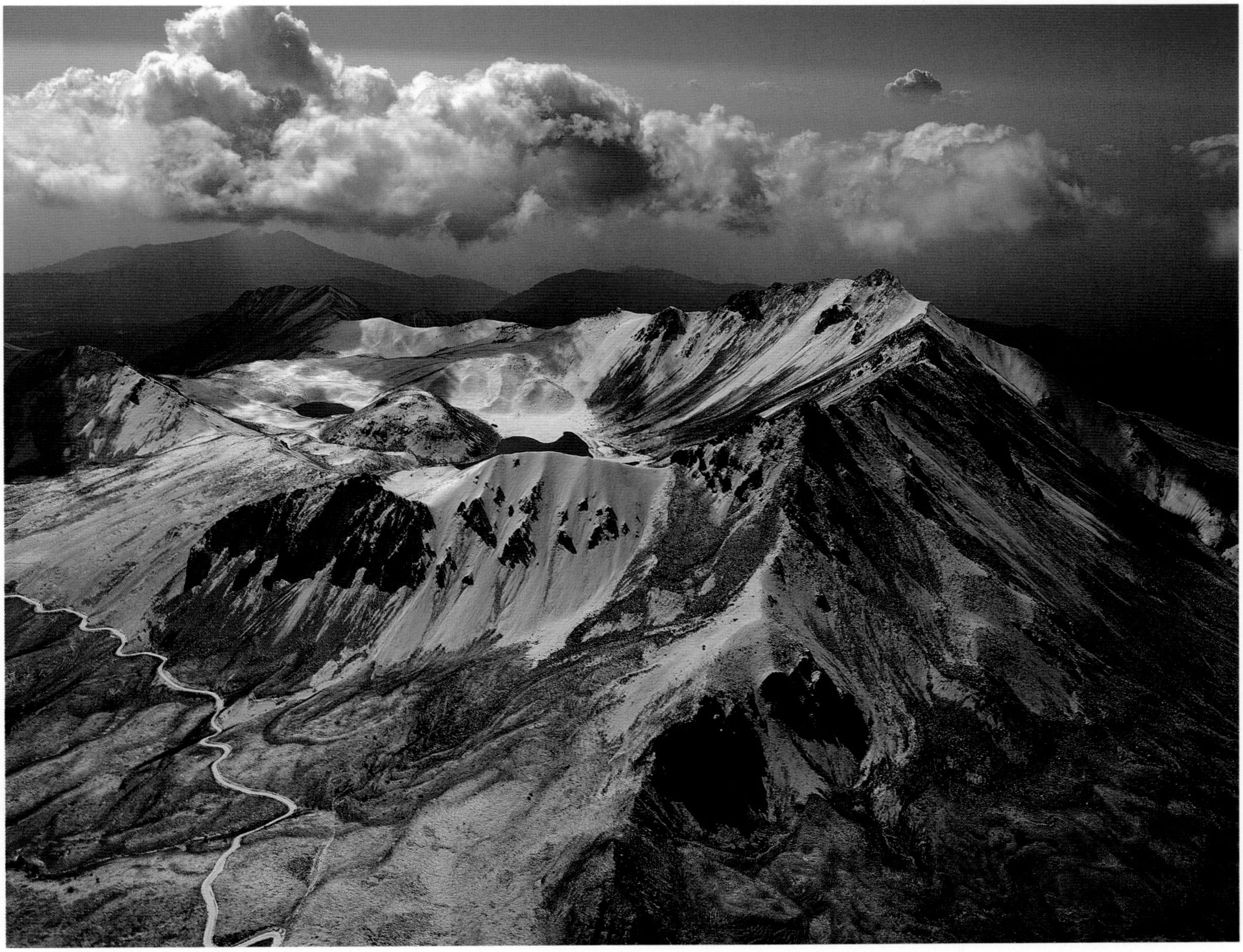

Winter snows crown the Nevado de Toluca volcano.

The Sun and Moon Lagoons in the crater of the Nevado de Toluca.

# MEXICO CITY

## The end of the fifth sun

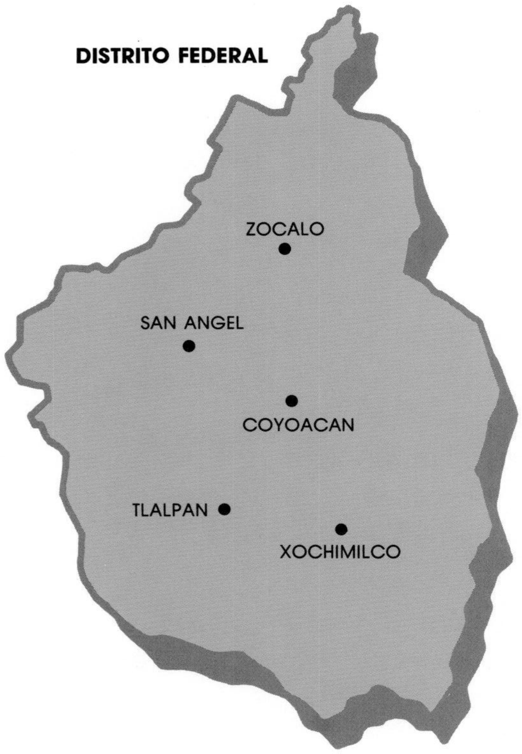


Forty million years ago, volcanos erupting along the southern edge of the central plateau of Mexico walled in an area of land about the size of Rhode Island. Without a river outlet, the valley steadily filled with water. By the time humans appeared on the American continent several shallow lakes had formed. Their marshy edges teemed with wildlife, and pine and oak woods covered the mountain slopes. At 7,000 feet, the valley enjoyed clear, crisp air. Summer rains replenished the lakes and winter nights were cold, but these were the only seasonal variations in an annual cycle of daily sunshine and light humidity.

Since the surrounding land lay above the water level, the water covering the valley floor could not be readily used to irrigate crops. The Indian tribes living on the shores of the lakes therefore improvised an ingenious system of cultivation. They floated giant reed baskets, filled with sand and mud dredged from the lake bottom, on the surface of the water. Under constant irrigation, these floating gardens, or *chinampas*, were extremely productive. Flowers and vegetables are still planted in the floating gardens of Xochimilco, today a southern suburb of Mexico City.

The *chinampas* were a key factor in the emergence of Mexico-Tenochtitlan, founded in 1325 by the Aztecs on an island west of the present Lake Texcoco. The town was originally a crowded refuge in the midst of the Aztec's better-established enemies; but just two hundred years later, the Spaniards encountered a city of exquisite beauty and precise order, set like a jewel amidst the blue lake waters. From Tenochtitlan, the Aztecs had come to rule an empire that encompassed most of pre-Columbian Mexico. However, their ruthless and violent reign created deep rifts within the ranks of the tributary states.

The conquistadors shrewdly exploited the potential for rebellion, and attacked Tenochtitlan at the head of a vast army of vengeful Indians. A two-month siege left the Aztec capital in ruins, its population decimated by famine and disease. Sensing the political importance of the site, Cortes insisted on rebuilding the city. The new houses and palaces were of European design, but the basic Aztec street grid laid out around a central square was retained.

*Trajineras*, or punts, await a busy Sunday morning in the canals of Xochimilco.

Paseo de la Reforma, once the Mayfair of Mexico City.

Itinerant street market sets up for the day.

The old quarter of Mexico City, built over the ruins of Tenochtitlan. ▶

A Diego Rivera fountain inspired by pre-Colombian myths.

Environmental sculpture amidst the lava fields of the University of Mexico campus.

The Palace of Chapultepec, surrounded by Chapultepec Park.

The open-air big cat cages at the zoo in Chapultepec Park.

Modern housing blocks encircle the Aztec pyramid and colonial church in Tlatelolco.

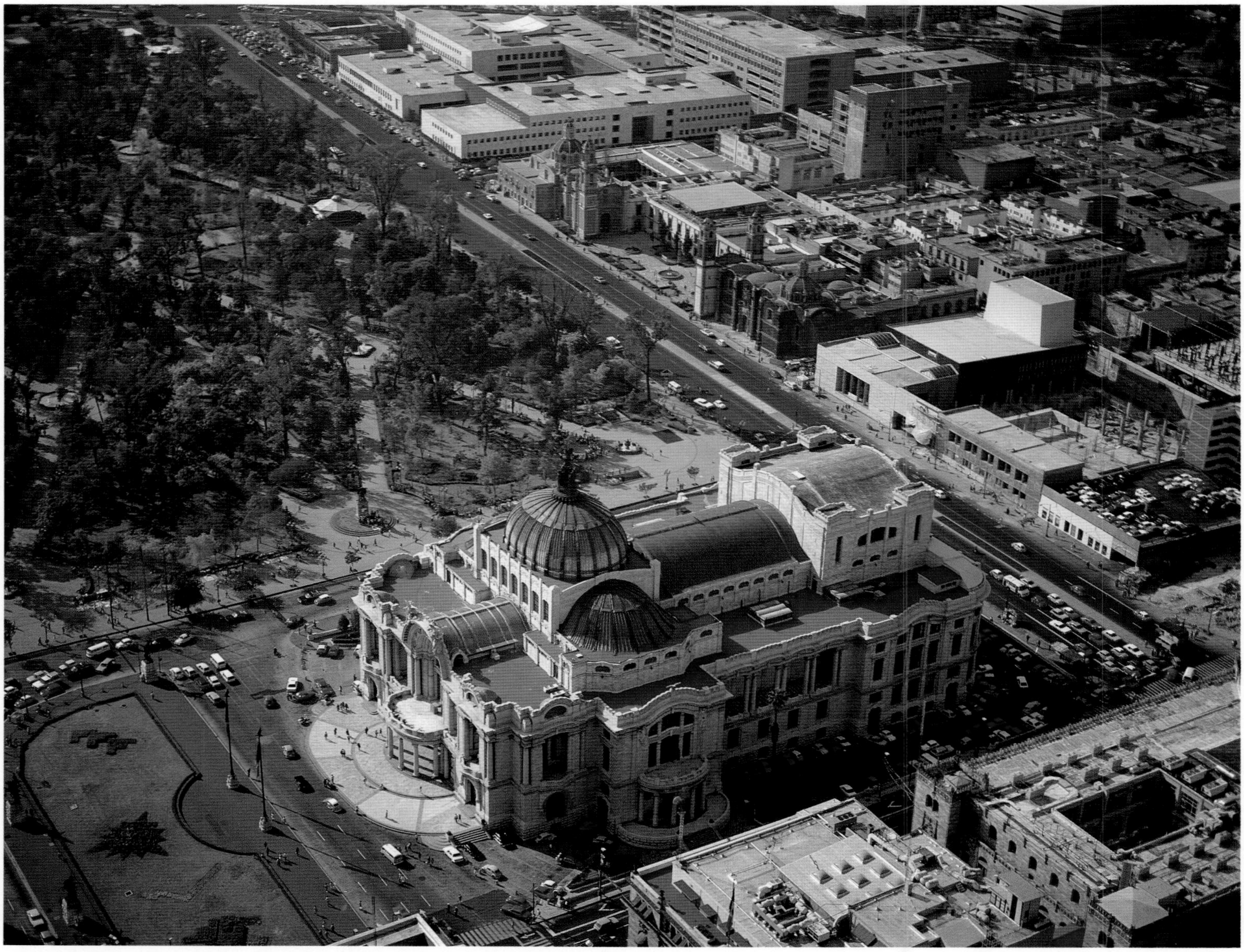

The Palace of Fine Arts, on the edge of the Alameda Park.

The Cathedral of the Virgin and the National Palace on the Zocalo square. ▶

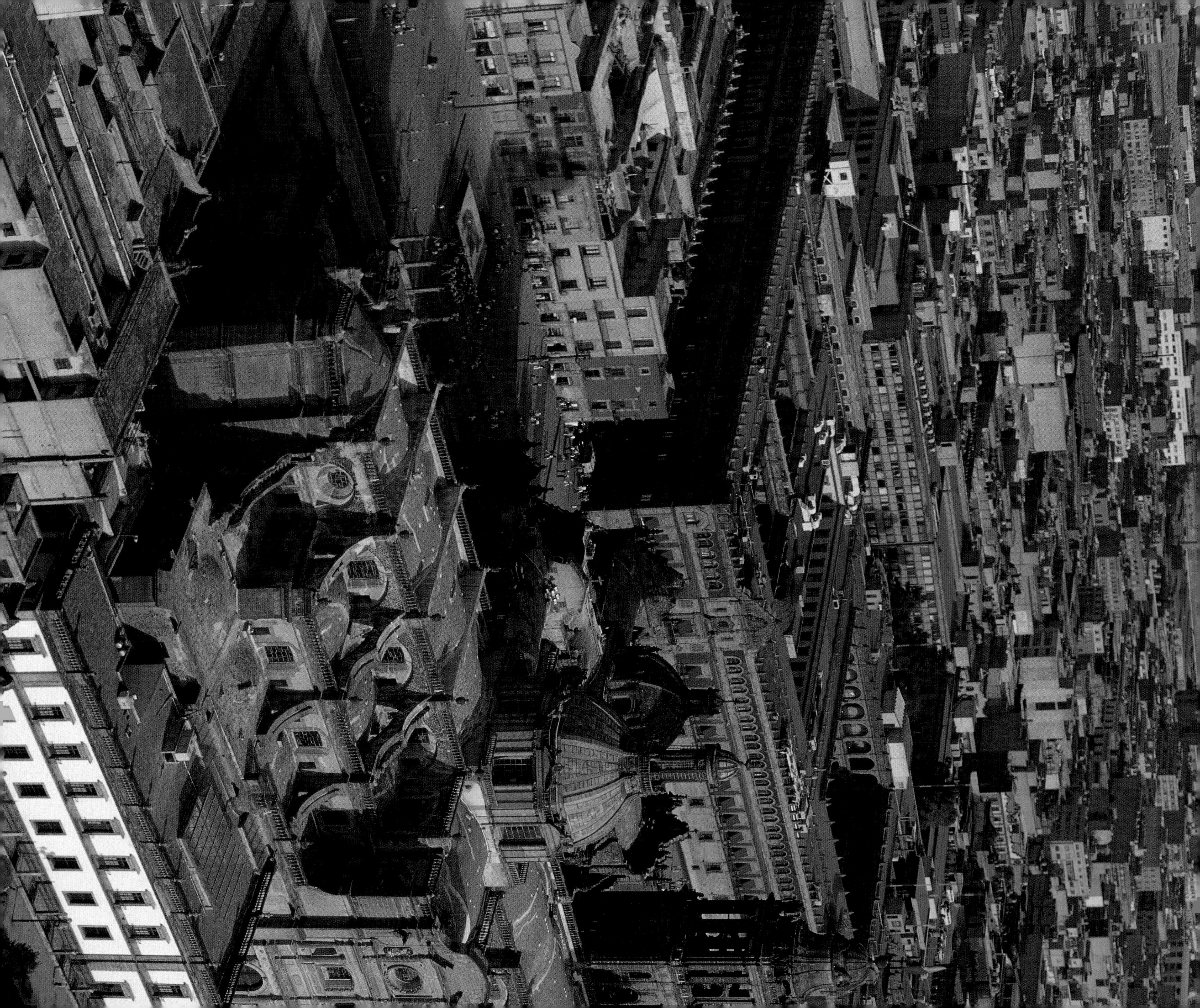

December 12th festivities at the shrine of Guadalupe.

Sculpture by Alexander Calder in the esplanade of the Azteca Stadium.

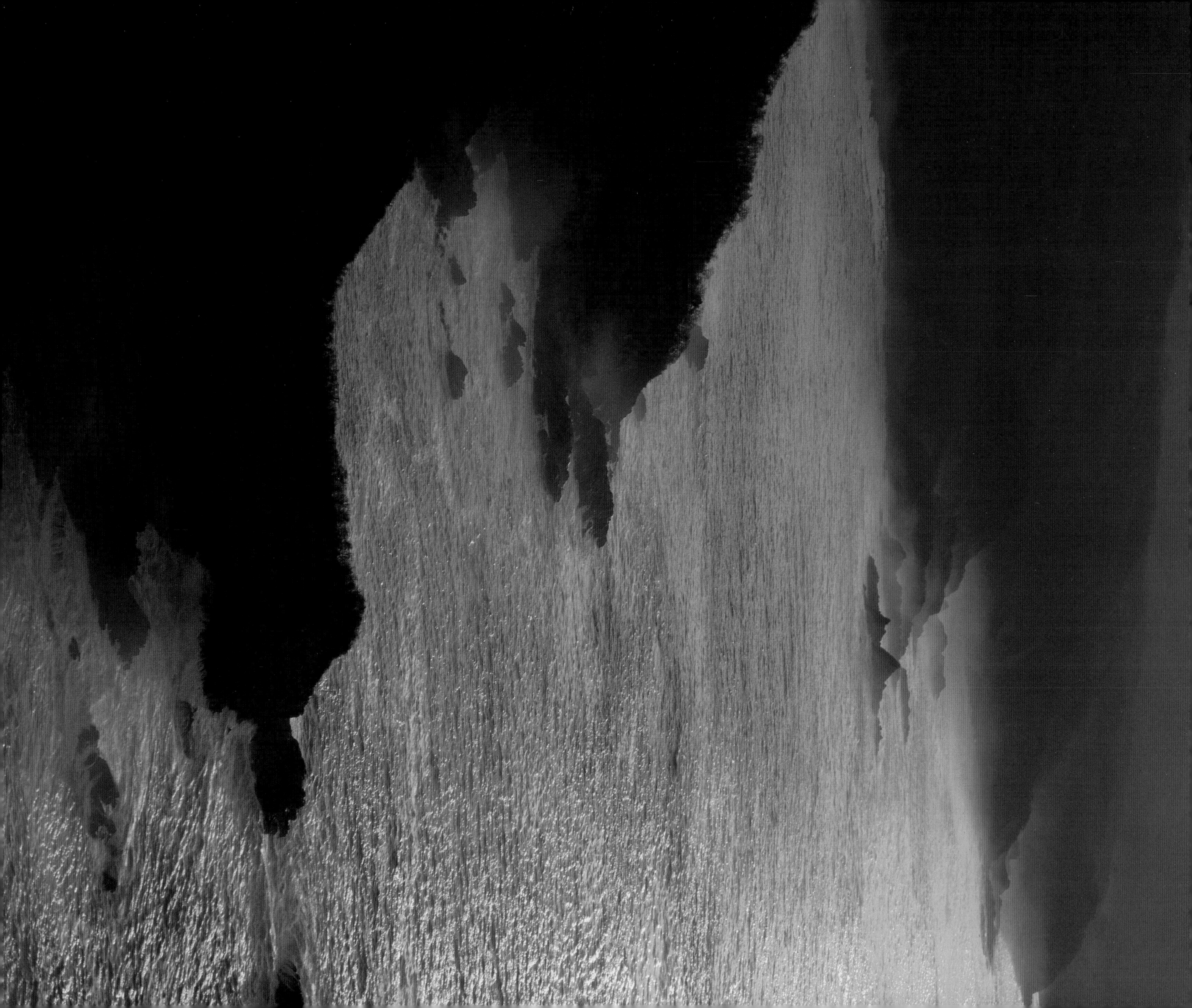

# THE PACIFIC COAST

## A golden shore

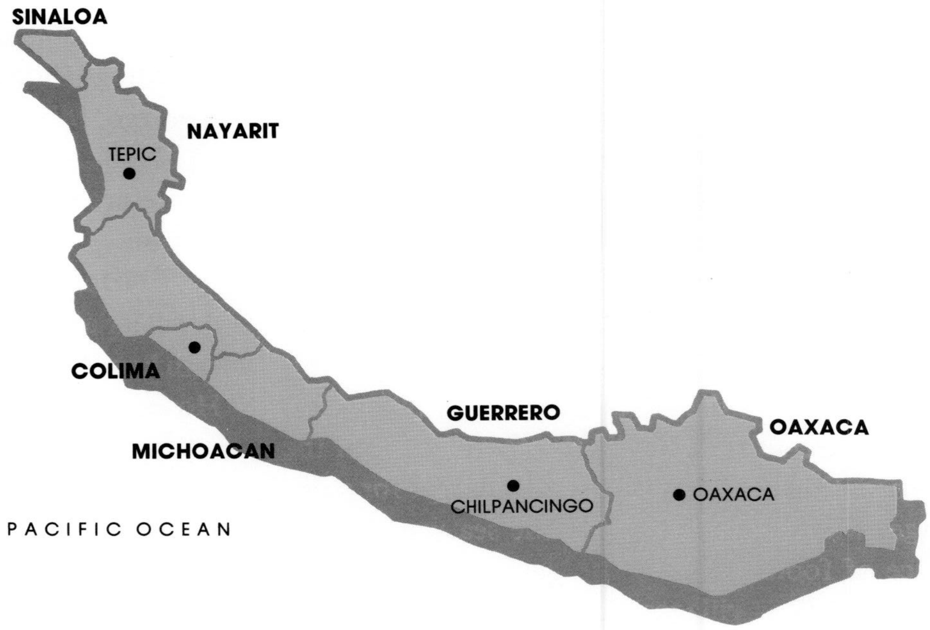


The topography along the Mexican Pacific Coast is remarkably similar to the shoreline from San Diego to Portland. The 1,100 mile stretch from Mazatlan to the Tehuantepec Isthmus is a changing landscape of shallow bays, sandy beaches, and cliffs which plunge into the sea. The real difference lies in the climate: while the sea in Portland could never be described as inviting and the winters are wet and cold, the sun shines upon the balmy Mexican Pacific nine days out of ten year-round.

Although there is little evidence of it today, a maritime story of global importance unfolded on the Mexican Pacific. When Columbus crossed the Atlantic in 1492 he hoped to re-establish the lucrative spice trade with the Far East via a new route to the west. The explorers who succeeded him were no less aware of the enormous benefits attached to such a discovery. The conquest of the Aztec empire enabled Hernan Cortes to dispatch expeditions to the southwestern seaboard where he planned to build ships. An early port at the mouth of the Balsas River was soon abandoned in favor of a new site on the broad and sheltered Bay of Santa Lucia. The Spaniards immediately laid out a rudimentary shipyard next to an Indian settlement called Acapulco.

Thus began the modern history of the most important port on the Pacific from the sixteenth to the eighteenth century. It was from Acapulco that Cortes sent troops to his cousin Francisco Pizarro who was embroiled in the conquest of Peru. The search for an interoceanic canal inspired expeditions from Acapulco to chart the west coast of America as far north as Prince William Sound in Alaska, where Valdez Port and Cordova Peak bear witness to the presence of Spanish-speaking explorers.

In 1559 King Philip II of Spain commissioned a fleet to conquer the Philippine Archipelago named after him and to chart the winds by which it might sail back to Acapulco. The navigator for the expedition, Andres de Urdaneta, a seasoned adventurer and Augustinian friar, plotted a northern course on the return journey to Mexico that took the fleet past San Francisco Bay. His observations served as the basis for the world's first book on navigation, printed in Mexico City in 1587. For two hundred and fifty years the Spanish galleons plied the trade route that connected Europe with the Orient. The armed fleet set sail from Acapulco loaded with cochineal and Mexican silver pesos —until the beginning of this century the most valued hard currency in China— and returned with cargos of ivory, silk, spices, and porcelain. Lured by the riches of the Orient, European pirates braved the stormy passage through the Strait of Magellan to prey upon the cargo vessels as they neared the Mexican coast.

Cliffs and waves outlined by the early morning sunlight, Michoacan.

Full moon rising over Acapulco and the Bay of Santa Lucia.





Small boats and bathers crowd the waters along Caleta Beach, Acapulco.

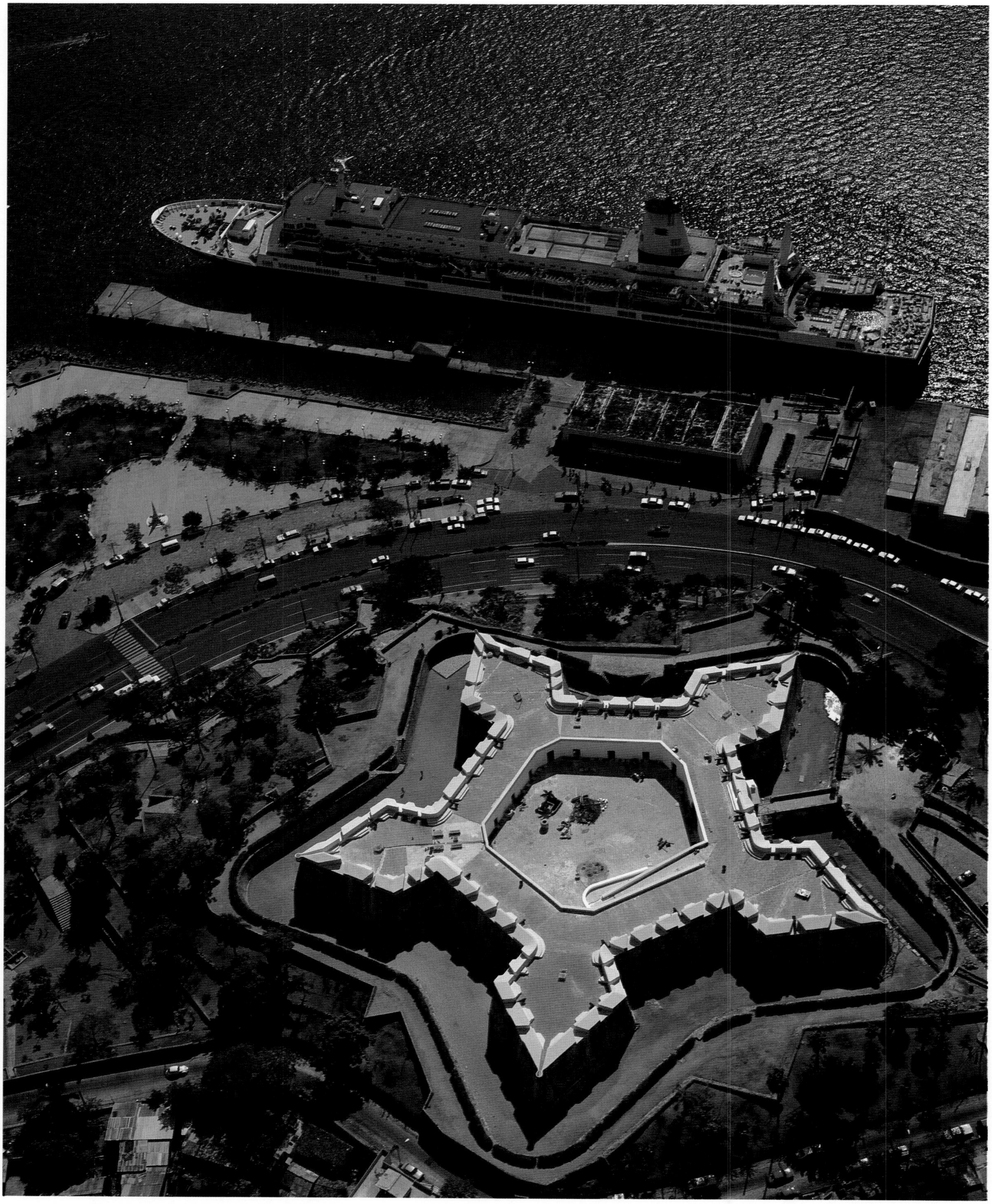

The Fort of San Diego watching over a cruise ship in Acapulco.

Fishing trawler stranded on the sands of Barra de Navidad, Jalisco.
Heavy waves break on the exposed rocks of the Jalisco coastline.



The Pitutina lighthouse overlooking Campos Cove, Michoacan.

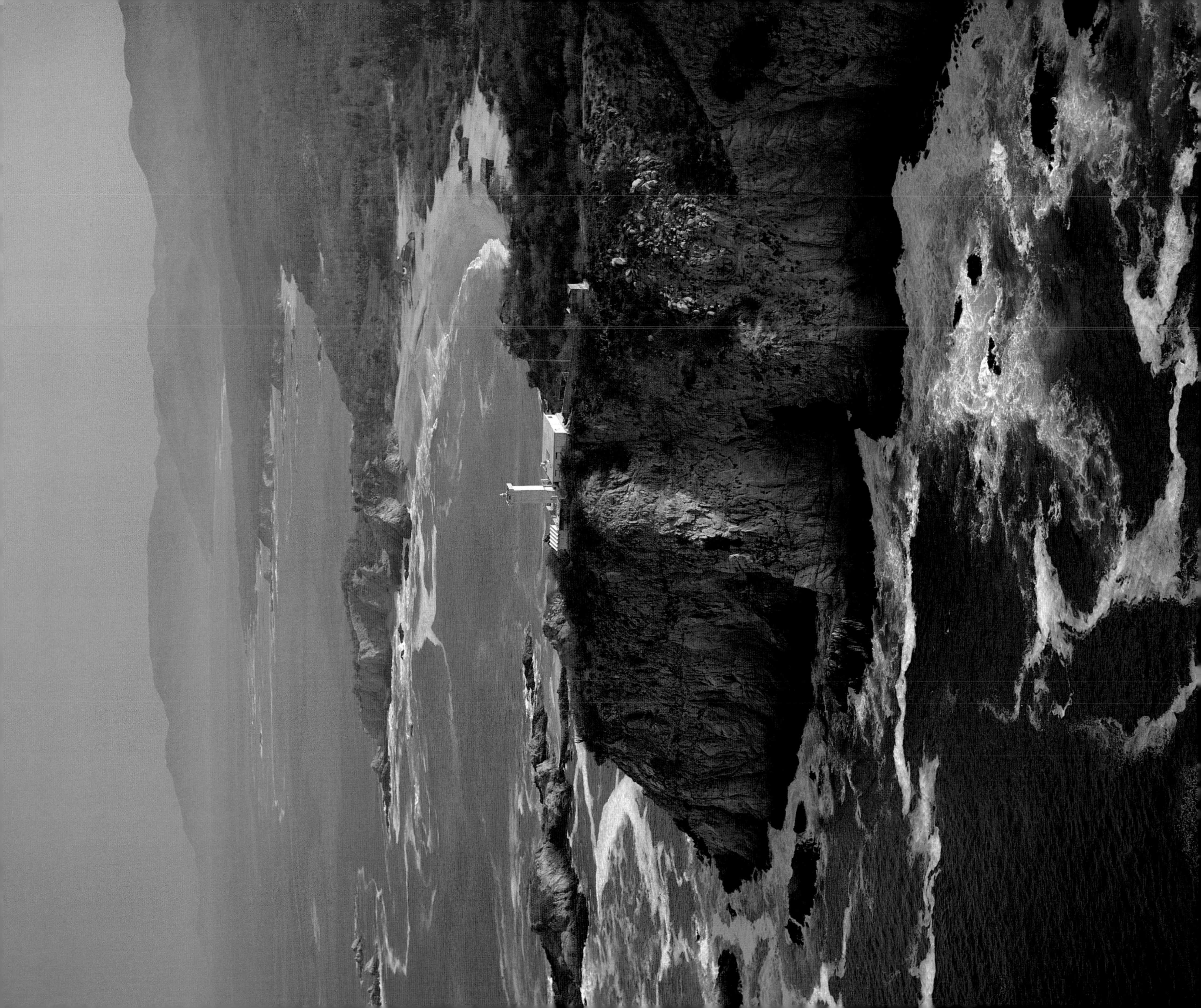

The Valley of Oaxaca on a clear afternoon before the summer rains.

The active Volcan de Fuego and the extinct Nevado de Colima, Jalisco.

The acropolis of Monte Alban overlooking the Valley of Oaxaca.▶

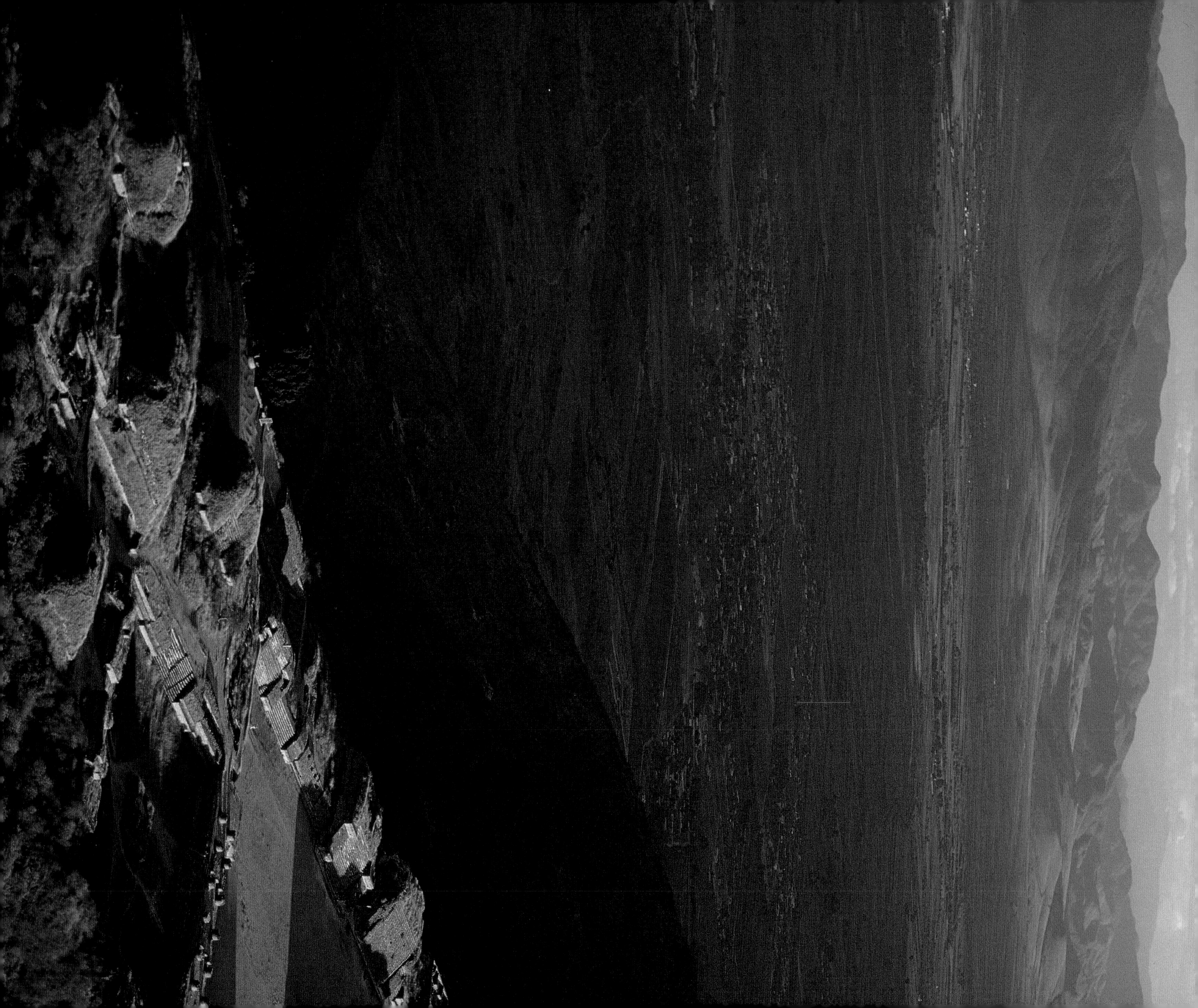

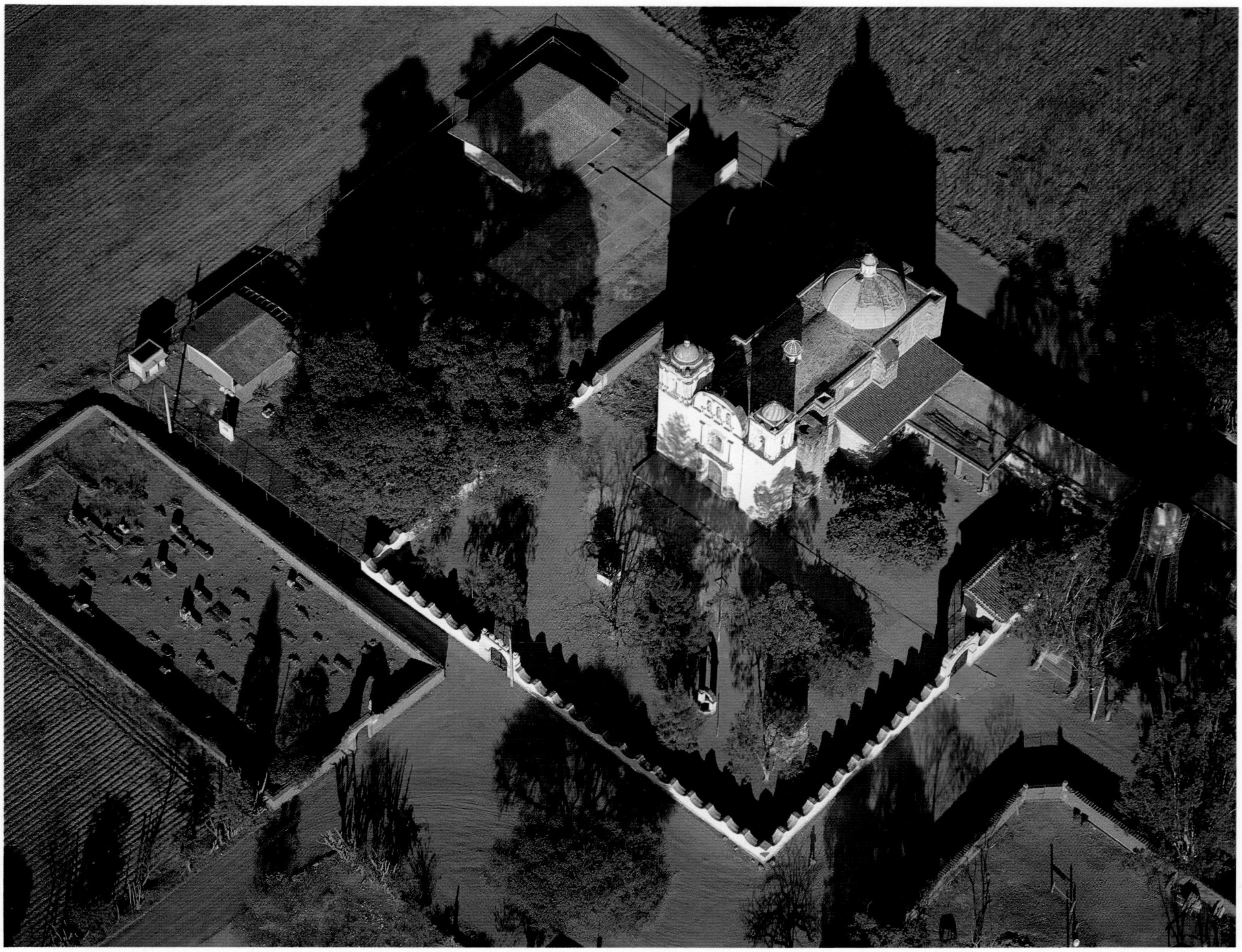

A country churchyard bougainvilla in the Valley of Oaxaca.

Fields of hibiscus in flower along the coast of Guerrero.

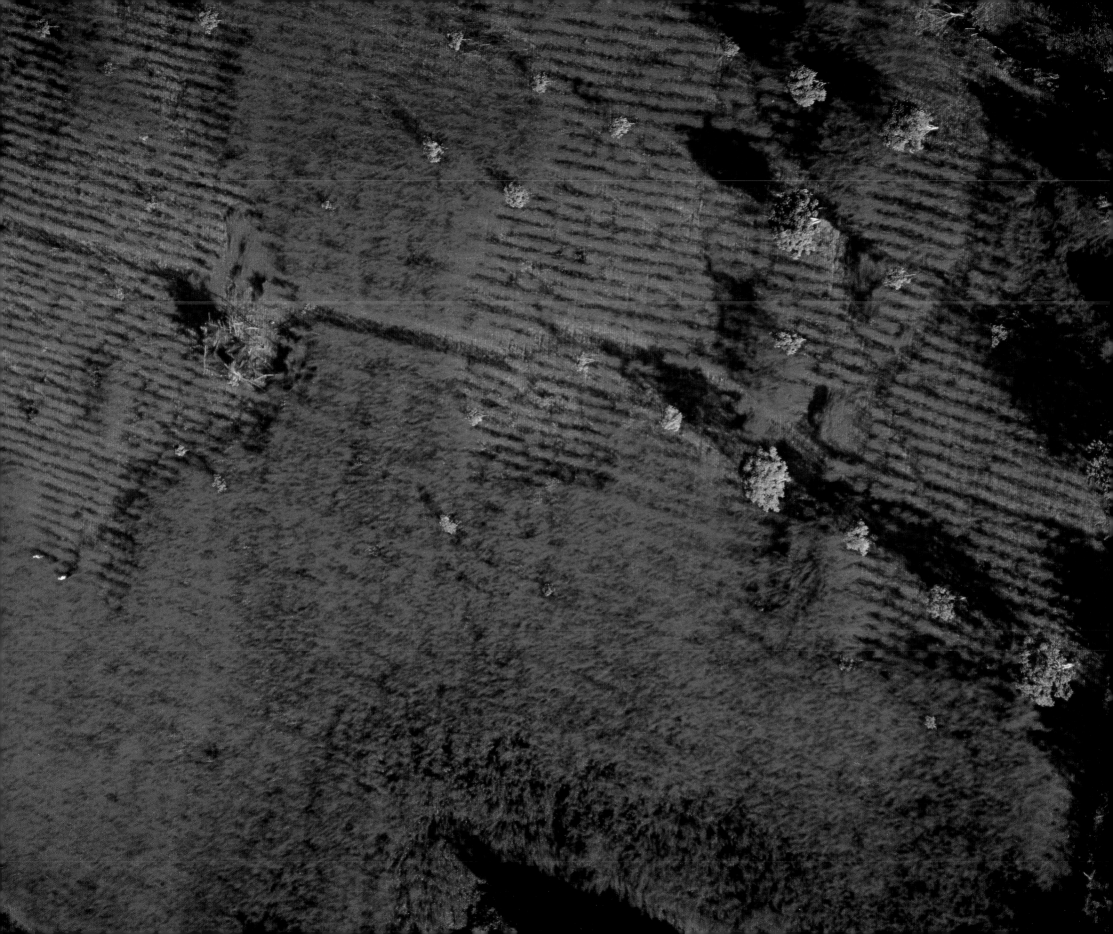

Palms and red earth characterize the Tierra Caliente of Oaxaca.

Sandbanks at a river mouth on the Oaxaca coastline.

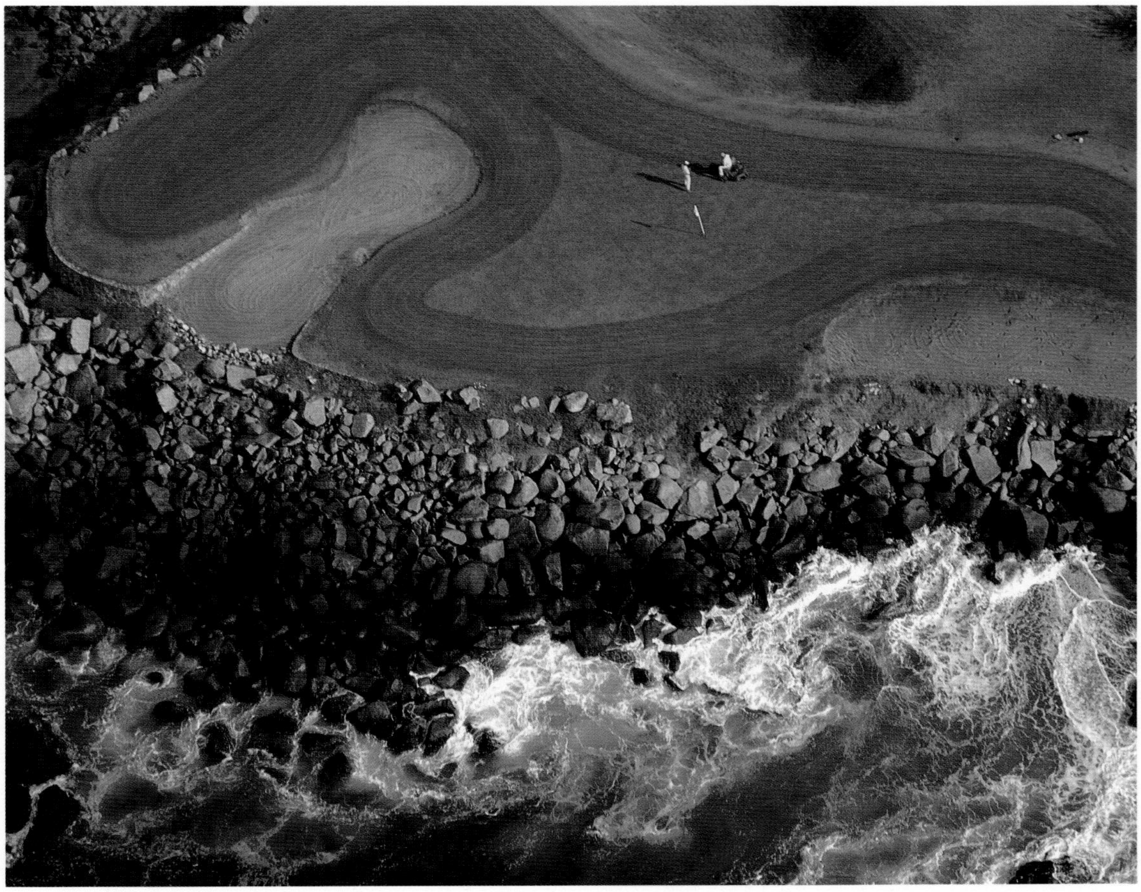

Oceanside twelfth hole on the Las Hadas golf course, Manzanillo.
Yacht flying a spinnaker off the coast of Mazatlan.

Moorish inspiration is evident in the resort village of Las Hadas, Manzanillo.

The coastal resort of Puerto Vallarta.

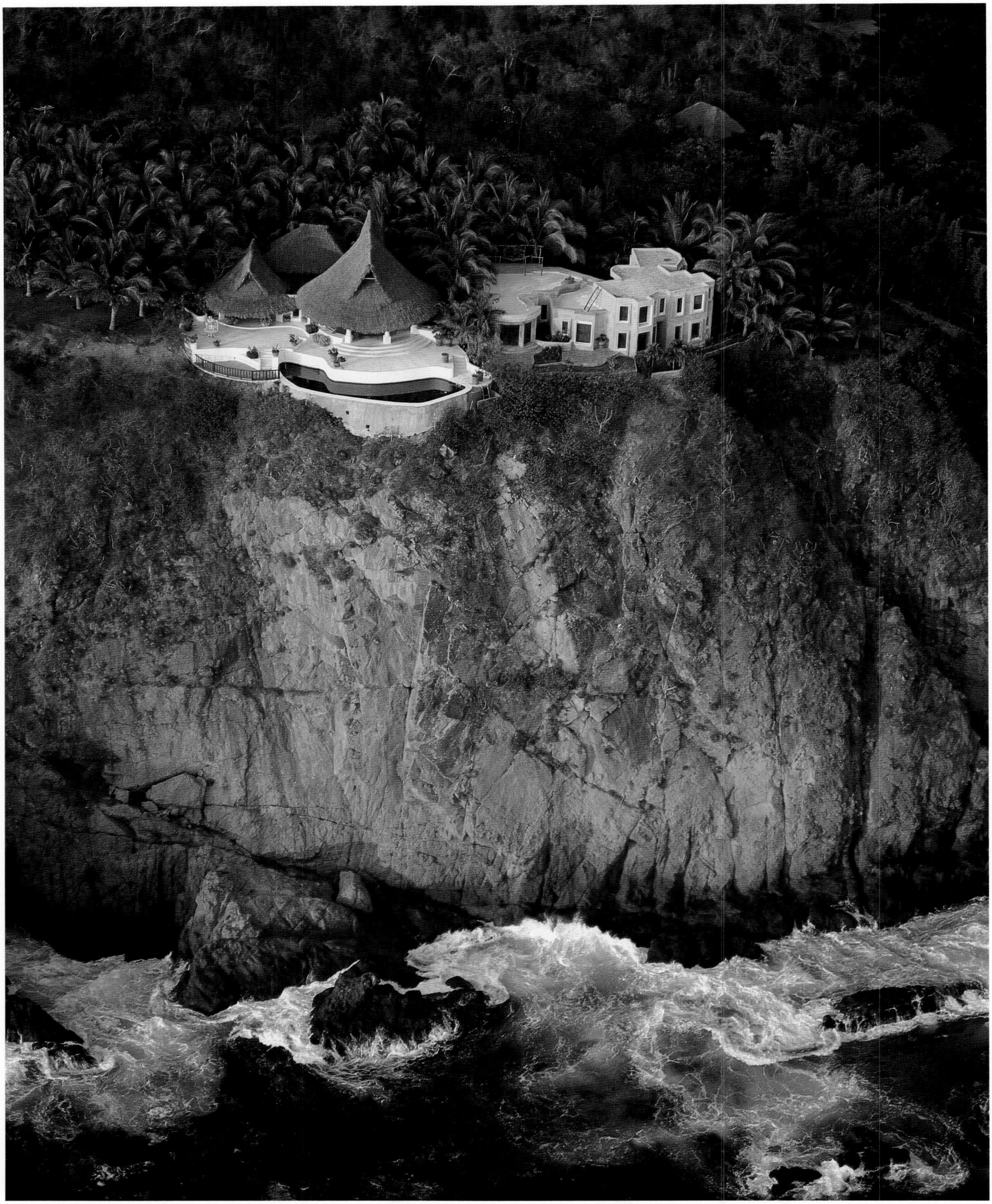

Seaside villa on the cliffs of Careyes, Jalisco.

Mexcaltitan, perhaps the original island home of the Aztecs.
Cows travel a watery path on their way home to Mexcaltitan.



Mangrove swamps near San Blas, Nayarit.

The traditional fishing town of Puerto Escondido, Oaxaca.

The port and tourist resort of Mazatlan.

# THE NORTHEAST

## From the silver cities to the Rio Grande

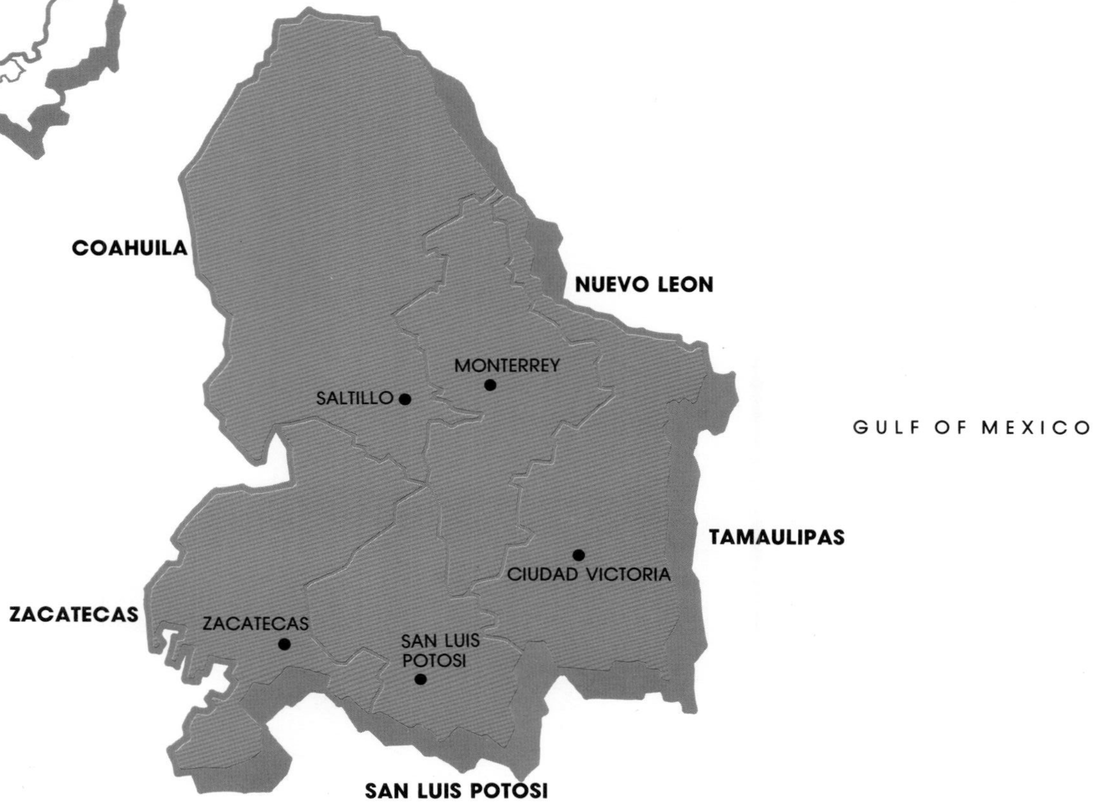


The landscape in the northern portion of Mexico is predominantly arid, a part of the broad swath containing the earth's great deserts that encircles the globe just to the north of the Tropic of Cancer. Lacking the benefits of large-scale irrigation, the pre-Columbian Indians of northern Mexico rarely established permanent settlements, but roamed the steppes in small bands. When the first Europeans explored the area, they found these tribes to be extremely warlike, and their initial efforts to dominate them proved largely unsuccessful.

Although the climate was cruel and the natives inhospitable, the conquistadors were motivated to persevere in trying to colonize this barren corner of the young Spanish Empire by the consuming desire to find precious metals. The discovery in 1546 of rich veins of silver within the Zacatecas mountains inspired teams of prospectors to seek their fortunes in the north. During the three hundred years that the Spanish imperial court ruled Mexico, life in the Northeast was conditioned by the settlers' determination to survive the climate, to wrest from the earth its mineral riches, and to subdue the Indian tribes with whom they fought for possession of the land.

Despite the tantalizing rewards, the colonization of this area of Mexico was slow. The prospectors were beset by many problems besides the natural environment and the natives. In most cases, they were inexperienced miners, unable to judge either the quality or quantity of the minerals on their claims. In fact, the silver content of the ore extracted was generally low, which made the mines costly to exploit. In the mid-sixteenth century, a brief expansion of large-scale silver mining resulted from the discovery of a refining process involving amalgamation with quicksilver. But the industry soon contracted when, in an effort to gain revenues, the Spanish Crown monopolized the supply of quicksilver and greatly inflated its price.

The situation began to change around 1750 when mining became a well organized business, partly through the introduction of Spanish legislation to support and regulate the silver trade, and partly because a Royal School of Mining was endowed to train engineers and geologists. By 1800 Mexico accounted for two thirds of the world's

Real de Catorce, ghost town, in the "Silver Belly" hills.

annual silver production. The German scientist and traveler, Baron von Humboldt, calculated that "the [annual] manufacture of silver from all the mines of Europe together would not keep the Mexican mint busy for more than fifteen days."

An array of mining camps grew up along the trails which branched off the winding road stretching from central Mexico north across the Rio Grande —or the Rio Bravo, as it is called in Mexico— as far as Santa Fe, New Mexico. Some of the trails along this "route of silver" led to camps which became cities, like San Luis Potosi or Saltillo. Other camps, like Real de Catorce, developed then became ghost towns as soon as the seams ran out or could no longer be mined profitably.

The apparent blessings of silver proved in the end to be a curse for both Spain and Mexico. Having used its riches to postpone industrialization, Spain was left behind by the progress of the modern world, and eventually succumbed to economic stagnation and social turmoil. In Mexico, wealth became so concentrated in the hands of the local aristocracy that Humboldt wrote in the early nineteenth century, "[Mexico is] the land of inequality."

The Spaniards' behavior towards the natives was not always prompted by greed and feelings of racial superiority. The desire of Christian missionaries to save souls also played a large part in the history of the region. In the early 1700's the Franciscan Friars from the Missionary Association in Zacatecas undertook a systematic campaign to evangelize and settle the native tribes. They traveled deep into the northern territories of New Spain, exploring the wilderness on both sides of the Rio Grande. The friars established a chain of missions along the river which served as a lifeline in a region almost devoid of water. Most of their settlements eventually succumbed to the perils of drought, disease, and Indian attack. But San Antonio, Texas, is an example of a town which grew out of a Franciscan mission that survived.

Following the Mexican-American War of 1847, Mexico lost its northern-most dominions and the Rio Grande was designated the boundary separating the two countries—two emerging nations with very different cultural and economic destinies. However, the issues which distance both governments have not prevented the development of a regional subculture among the people living along the border river. In recent years the evolution of a lifestyle which transcends the frontier has become evident. The intercultural exchange is most apparent in the use of language, with ordinary speech comprised of both Spanish and English vocabularies, and in cooking, where typical Mexican ingredients spice up traditional American dishes.

The people of northeastern Mexico are renowned for being enterprising and forthright. Their tendency to frugality, probably a natural reaction to their barren surroundings, is not easily understood by the rest of Mexico, where nature has been more generous. Nonetheless, the sustained industrial development of the city of Monterrey is a clear example of northern business instinct. Founded in the foothills of the Sierra Madre in 1596, the city remained a small frontier community until the end of the nineteenth century. Today Monterrey is Mexico's third largest city and its mightiest industrial center.

According to local lore, Monterrey owes its transformation to a brewery. Beer needs bottles, so a glass factory was soon in operation. The bottles had to be capped, and a foundry followed suit. Boxes were indispensable for the shipment of beer, so a cardboard mill resulted. So the industrial revolution came to Monterrey.

Political stability at the turn of the century, the construction of railroads to the expanding American market, and the arrival of foreign investment were the main elements that consolidated Monterrey's position as a modern business center. The city's factories now account for about 25% of the entire industrial output of the nation, while its dynamic and progressive corporations occasionally figure among the Fortune 500.

Environmental conditions no longer inhibit progress in the northeast of Mexico. The mining of iron and coal, the fuel of industrial development, has replaced the silver industry. Irrigation projects have enlarged the areas of farmland, which produce large crops of sorghum, citrus fruits, grapes, and cotton. Modern farm tools have been able to work the previously barren land where hand tools could barely scratch the surface.

Despite the economic progress of this area of Mexico, the disparity between Mexico and the United States is a constant factor in the cultural environment, particularly along the two-named river frontier—is it the Rio Bravo or the Rio Grande? One wonders if the modern industrial age will provide future generations with a compensatory aesthetic legacy of comparable value to the gracious beauty of colonial architecture. Perhaps the lore and lingo and the *arte culinario* of the border will be the legacy of our time.



The mouth of the Rio Grande River on the Gulf of Mexico.

Saddle Mountain dominates the cityscape of Monterrey.

A *campesino* village on the plains of Zacatecas.

Sandstone cliffs in the Sierra del Carmen, Coahuila.

The evening sky of Zacatecas reflected in a country pond.

The mining city of Zacatecas clustered around a Baroque cathedral. ▶

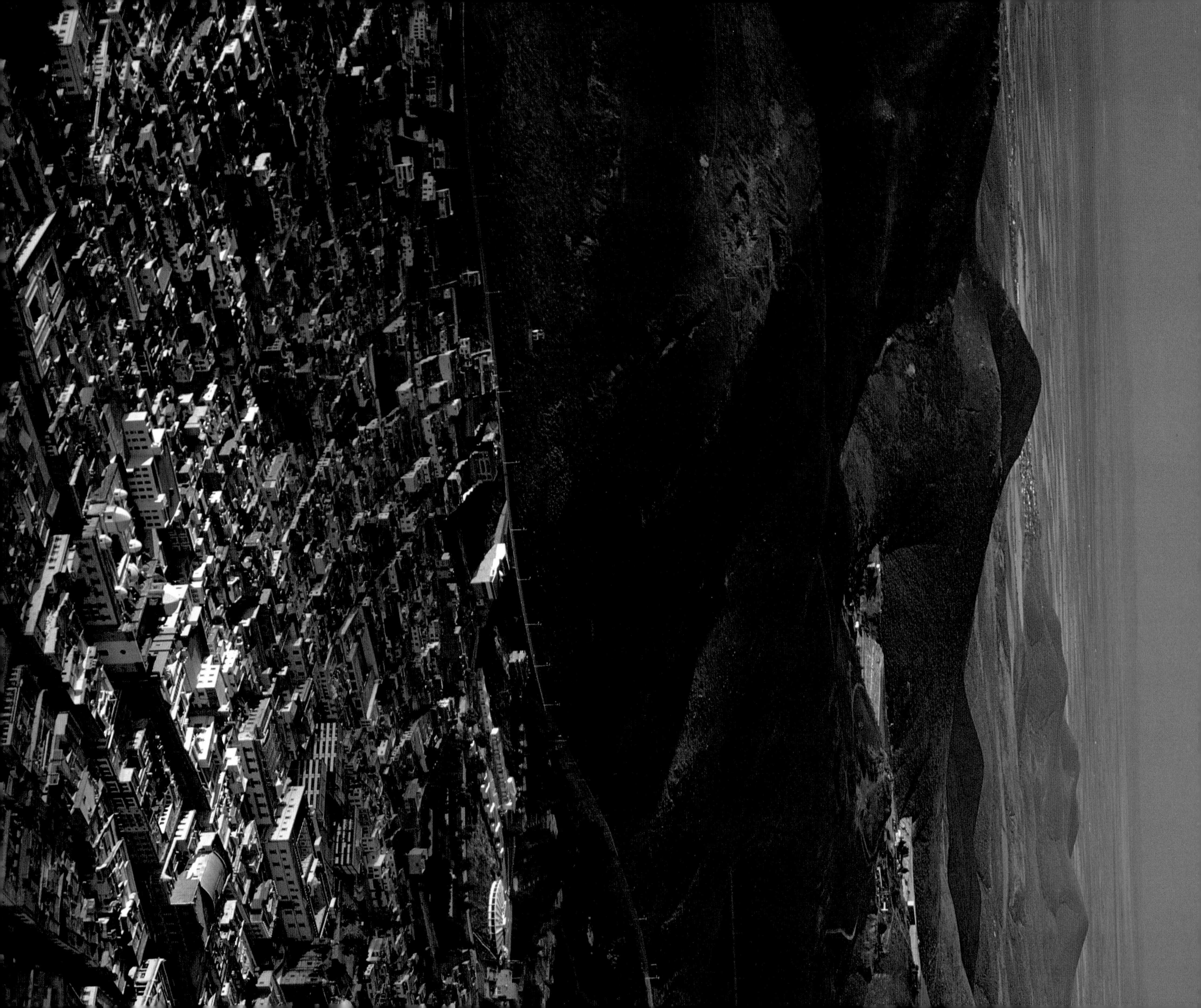

Traditional shrimp boats in the Laguna Madre.

A one hundred mile sand bar divides the Laguna Madre from the Gulf of Mexico.

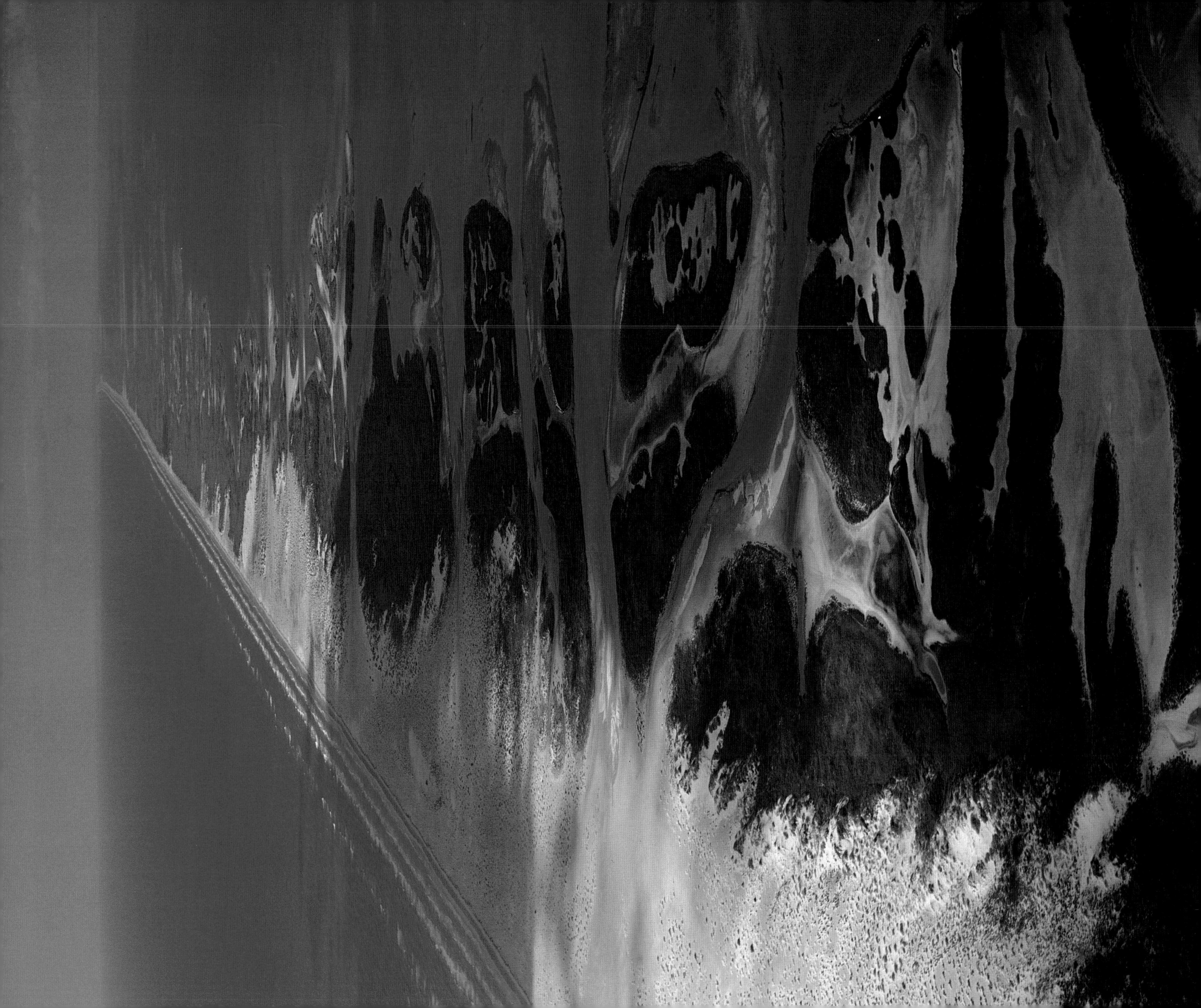

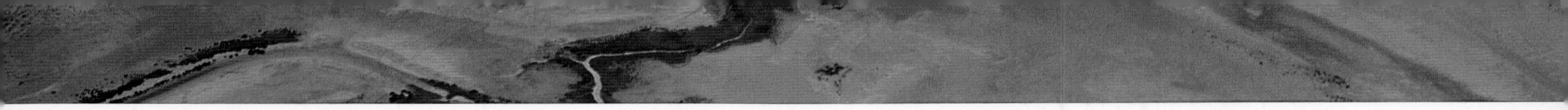

# THE NORTHWEST

## Wilderness and revolution

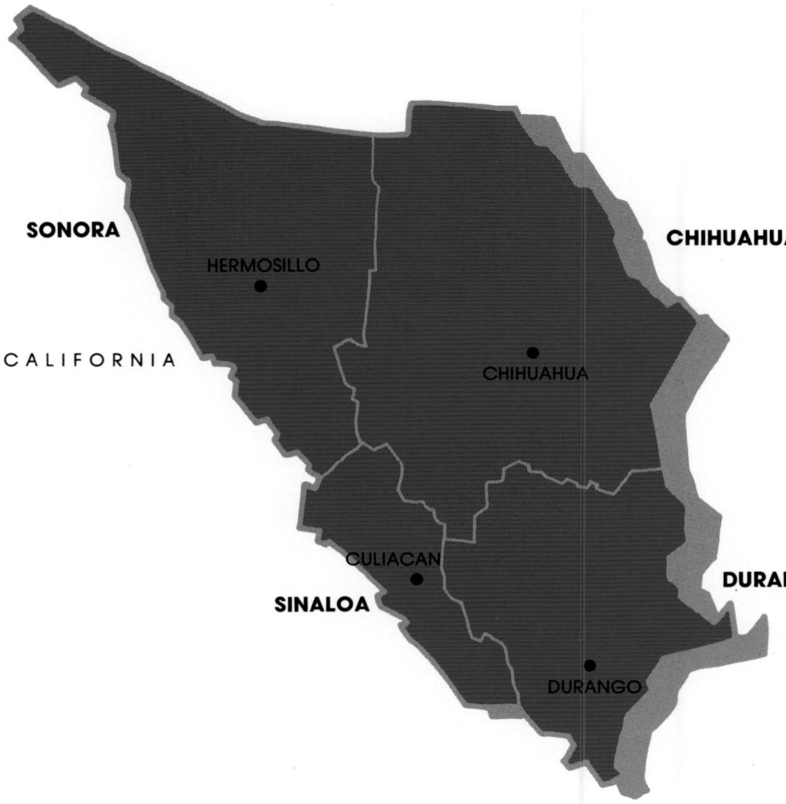


The northwestern portion of Mexico is to the rest of the country what Texas is to the United States: rough-hewn, expansive, larger than life. Compared to the gradual stairway climb from the eastern coastal plain to the central plateau, the abrupt ascent from the Sea of Cortes to the northwestern highlands seems more like a sheer wall. The Sierra Madre Occidental is so rugged that only one paved road and a single-track railway connect the interior of the country with the northwestern coast. Even today the road is so steep that a traveler must approach it with the courage of a medieval knight about to scale a fortress wall. The Sierra rises to peaks of over 9,000 feet and then tumbles into gorges like the Barranca del Cobre, which is deeper than the Grand Canyon. The flatlands of the Northwest present their own formidable barriers to human habitation. About 150 miles south of the Arizona border, the irrigated coastal plain disappears into the Altar Desert, a wilderness as big as Vermont and as dry as the Sahara.

In addition to the ruggedness of the terrain, the sheer size of the Northwest is in itself a barrier to communication with the rest of the country. The state of Chihuahua alone, which is less than half of the region, comprises more territory than Great Britain.

The scarcity of water on the northern plains rarely allowed the early inhabitants to settle permanently. However, during the first half of the thirteenth century, a well-planned town flourished in the valley of the Casas Grandes River. Archeological exploration of the ruins has shown that the irrigation system surrounding the town served also to pipe running water through a series of underground channels into the communal dwelling units. The town of Casas Grandes must once have looked like the Pueblo Indian towns of New Mexico. Rising as high as five stories above ground level, the houses were organized around open courtyards. Walls were made of clay poured into sliding forms, a technique similar to that used for modern concrete buildings. By the end of the fifteenth century, when Columbus sailed the Atlantic, the site was inhabited only by small groups of hunters, unaware of the civilization that had preceded them.

Alvar Nuñez Cabeza de Vaca, the redoubtable

The Barranca del Cobre canyon in Chihuahua.

Wheat fields harvested by the Menonite farm colonies of Chihuahua.





A stream brings life to the salt flats of Altata Bay, Sinaloa.

Hacienda dominated by its chapel on the plains of Chihuahua.

Rocas de Lumbre, or Rocks of Fire, Chihuahua. ▶

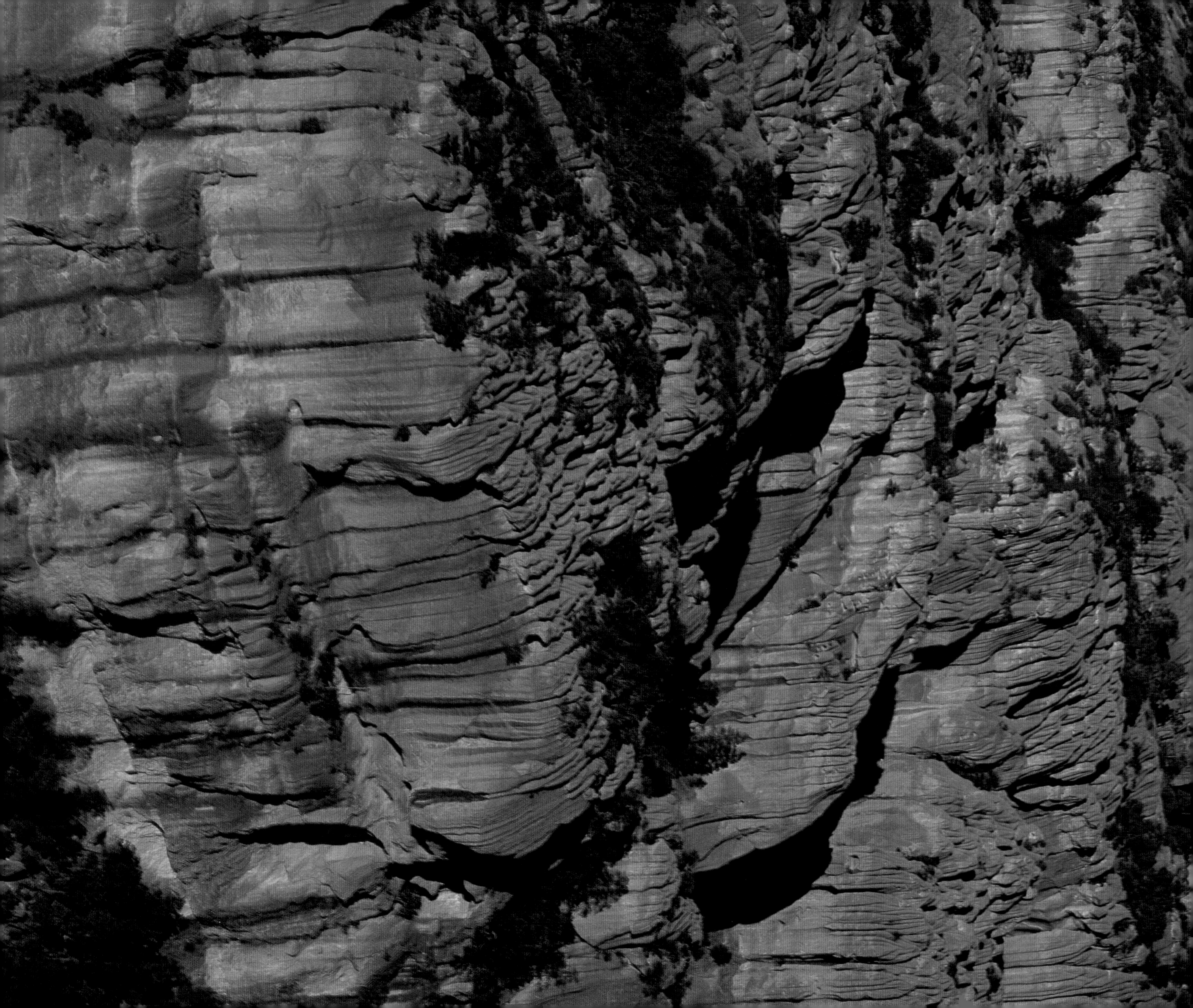

The headwaters of the Conchos River, Chihuahua.

Autumn colors in the birch woods of Chihuahua.

The clay remains of Casas Grandes, ancient town of the Chihuahuan Desert.

Modern highrises have changed the cityscape of old Chihuahua.

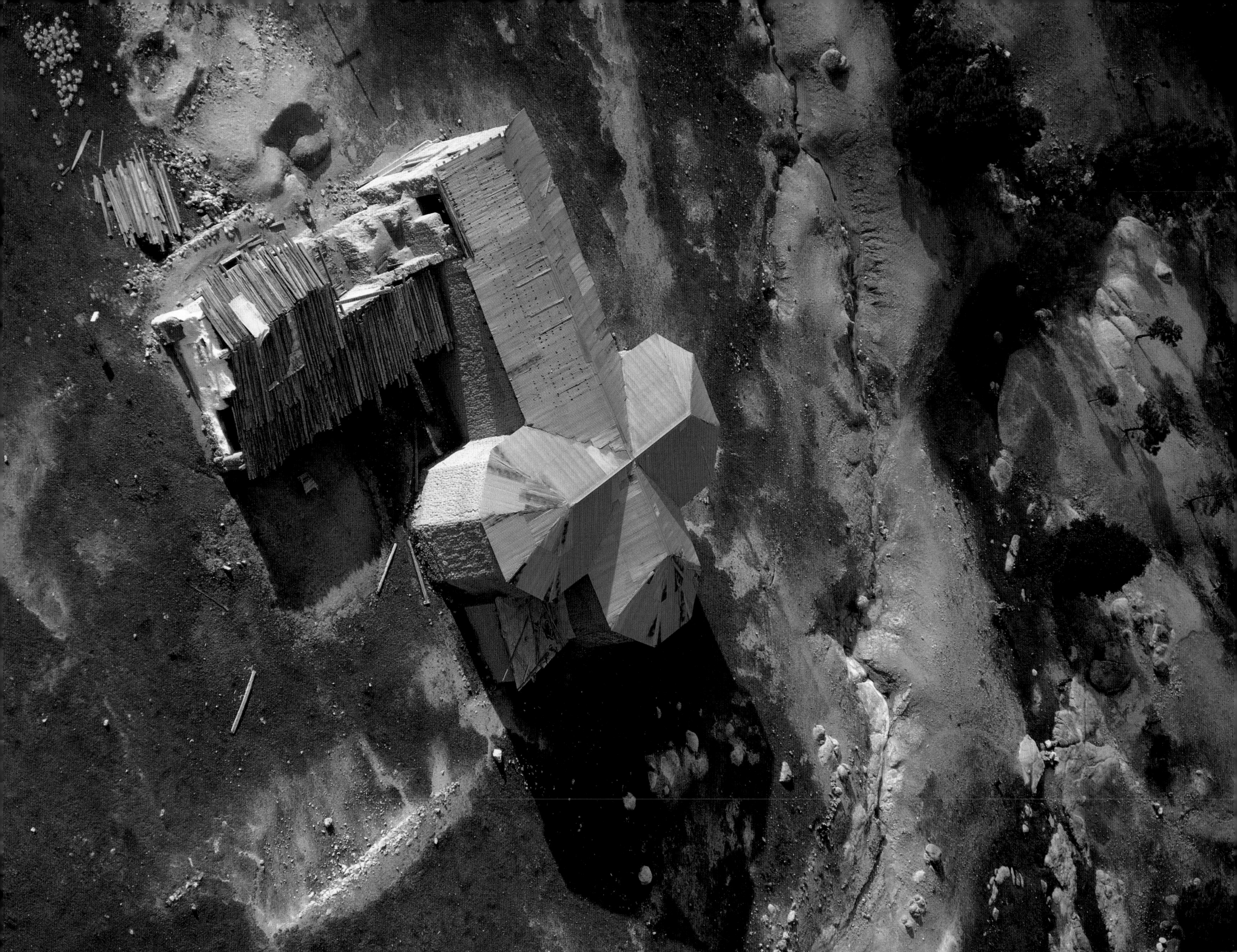

A rural train bound for Ciudad Juarez crosses the Chihuahuan plains.
Pelicans on the Abelardo Rodriguez Reservoir, Hermosillo, Sonora.

Tarahumara Indian church in the canyon region of Chihuahua.

Fishing boats moored to a central buoy in the harbor of Puerto Peñasco, Sonora.

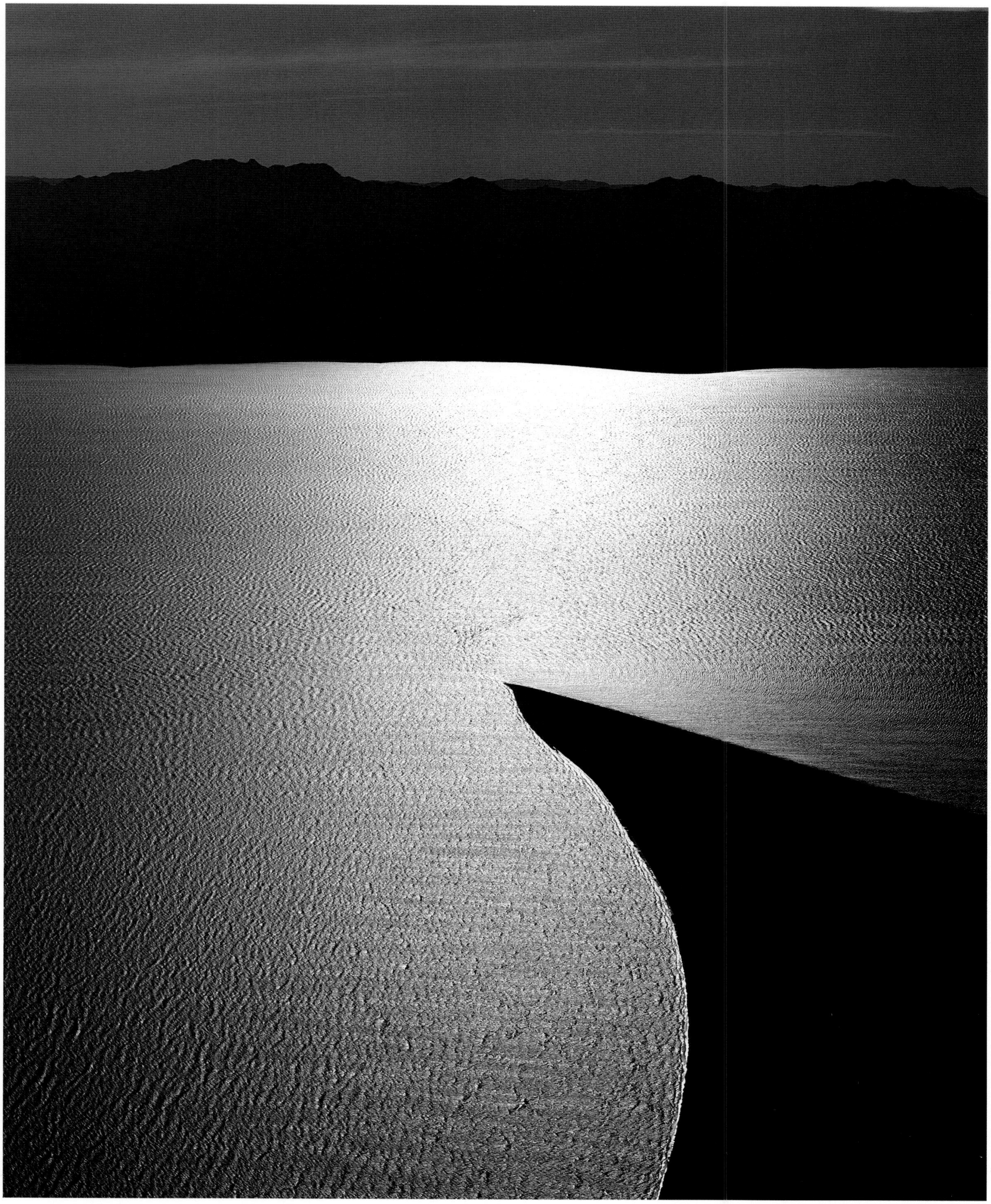

The Infiernillo Straits separate Isla Tiburon form the Sonora coast.

An extinct volcano in the Cerro del Pinacate National Park, Sonora.

Volcanic outcrops of the Altar Desert blaze in the early morning sun.

The Basaseachic Waterfall in the mountains of Chihuahua.

The Sierra del Nido rises abruptly from the Chihuahuan prairie.

# BAJA CALIFORNIA

## A hostile beauty

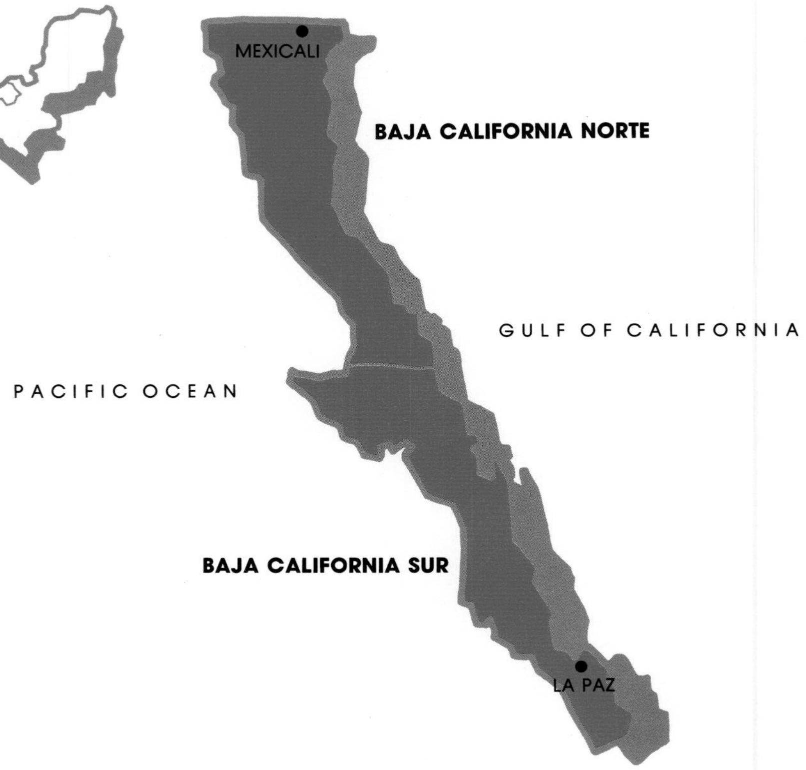


Baja California remains one of the loneliest regions on the American continent even though it lies just to the south of one of its most densely populated areas. Its lack of human settlement cannot be attributed to remoteness or inaccessibility since there is hardly a spot on the peninsula more than 40 miles from the coast. Neither does want of potential material rewards account for the absence of people. Quite to the contrary; the uninterrupted, 750 mile-long mountain range running from one end of the peninsula to the other has lured numerous adventurers and prospectors in search of mineral deposits potentially as rich as those to be found in other parts of Mexico.

The desolation of Baja California can be attributed more to its climate, which resists human settlement. At the northern and southern extremes there is a regular rainy season, but most of the peninsula goes for months, even years, without a single drop from the sky. In these areas, whatever rain there is falls mostly in storms that go as suddenly as they come. Absence of water prevents the growth of vegetation, and absence of vegetation prevents the buildup of a water-absorbent soil that might sustain more vegetation or prevent the water from tumbling precipitously into the sea or some salty lagoon to evaporate under the sun.

Only a minimum of this water can be absorbed by the plants that have adapted to the environment, mostly an astonishing variety of cactuses. Each downpour is celebrated with an outburst of blooms. After rain, the predominantly tawny landscapes are suddenly graced with streaks of brightly colored flowers, but it is only a matter of a few days before the relentless sunshine burns everything back to its usual desolate appearance. Adaptation of plants and animals to the particular conditions in Baja California has been so specific that certain species depend on conditions peculiar to the locale for their very survival.

In satellite photos the crooked coastline of Baja California usually appears without haze or humidity to blur any detail, illustrating that this is one of the most consistently cloudless places on the globe. The daily presence of solar heat evaporates great amounts of surface water from the Sea of Cortes (Gulf of California) that separates Baja California from the mainland of Mexico. To compensate for that loss, a deep current of water enters the gulf from the Pacific Ocean. Rich in nutrients, this cold seawater turns the gulf into the most productive commercial fish-

Sandbanks in Balandra Bay, Baja California Sur.

Isla Espiritu Santo, Baja California Sur.



on maps drawn almost 150 years later. According to the



Sand and vegetation meet at Santa Maria Bay.

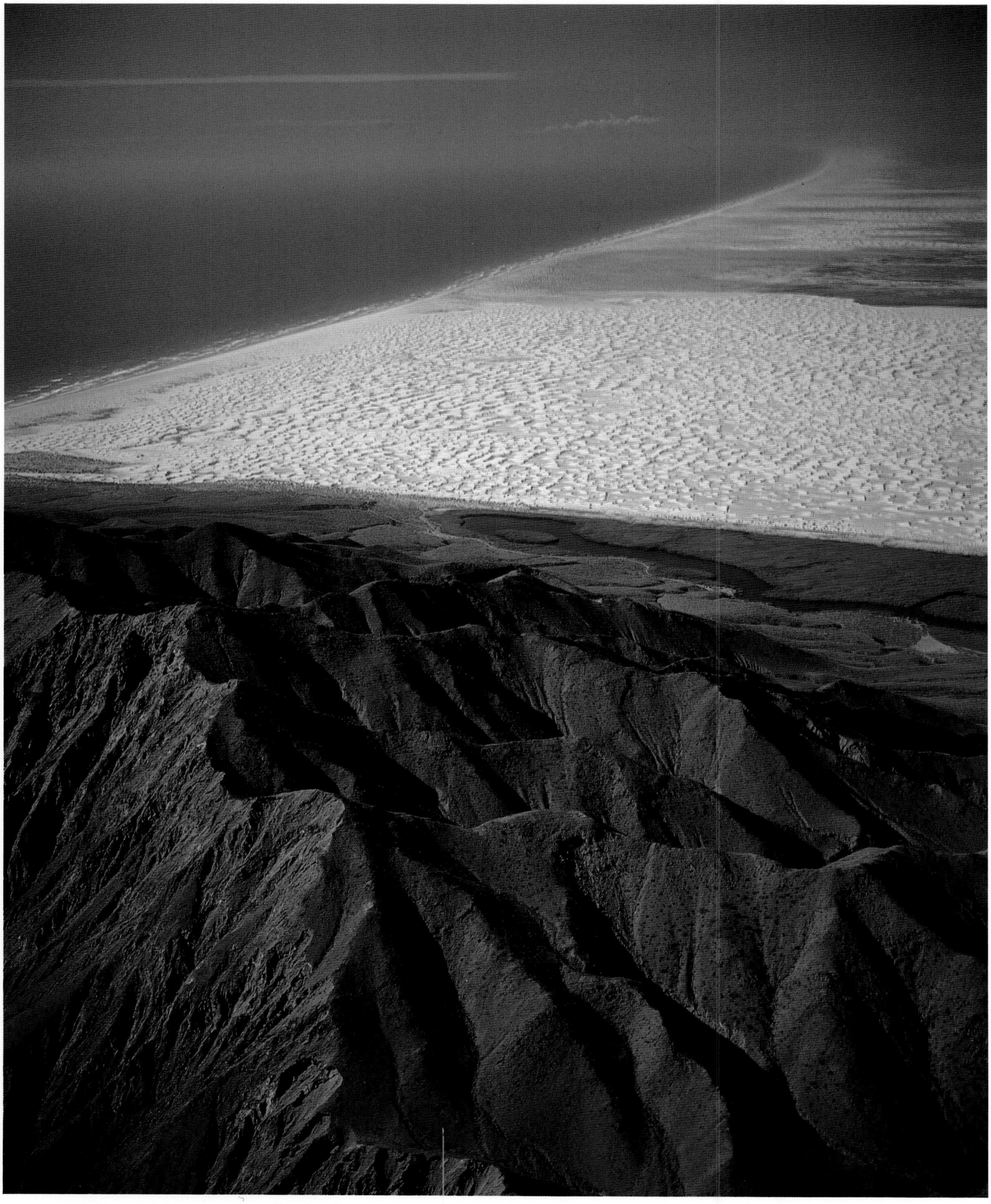

San Lazaro Mountains at the tip of Isla Magdalena.

Early morning fishing launches, Cabo San Lucas.



Land's end at Cabo San Lucas.

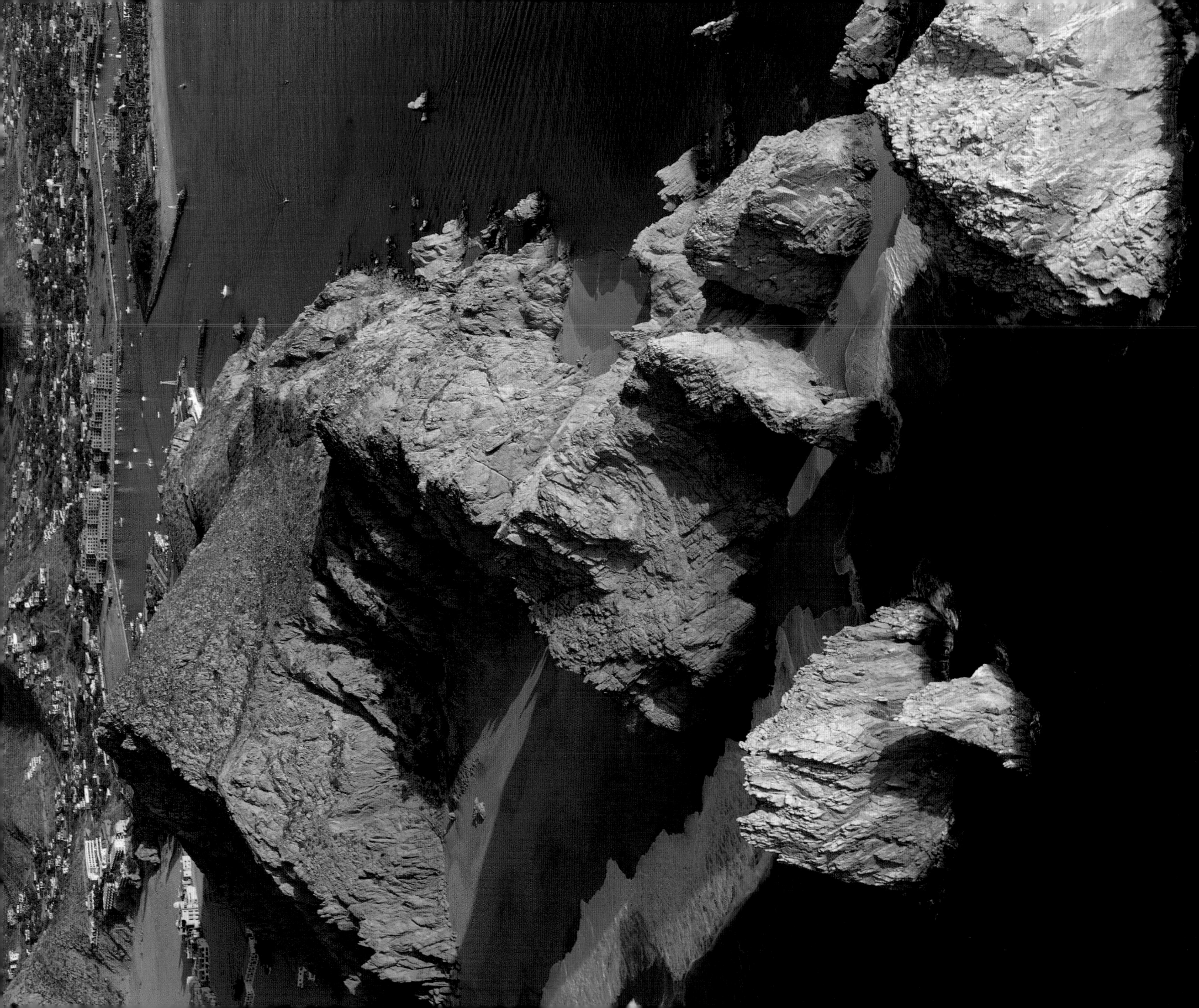

An isolated farmstead on the northern Pacific coast of Baja California.

Isla San Francisquito in the Sea of Cortes.

Winter plowing by the Pacific, Santo Tomas. ▶

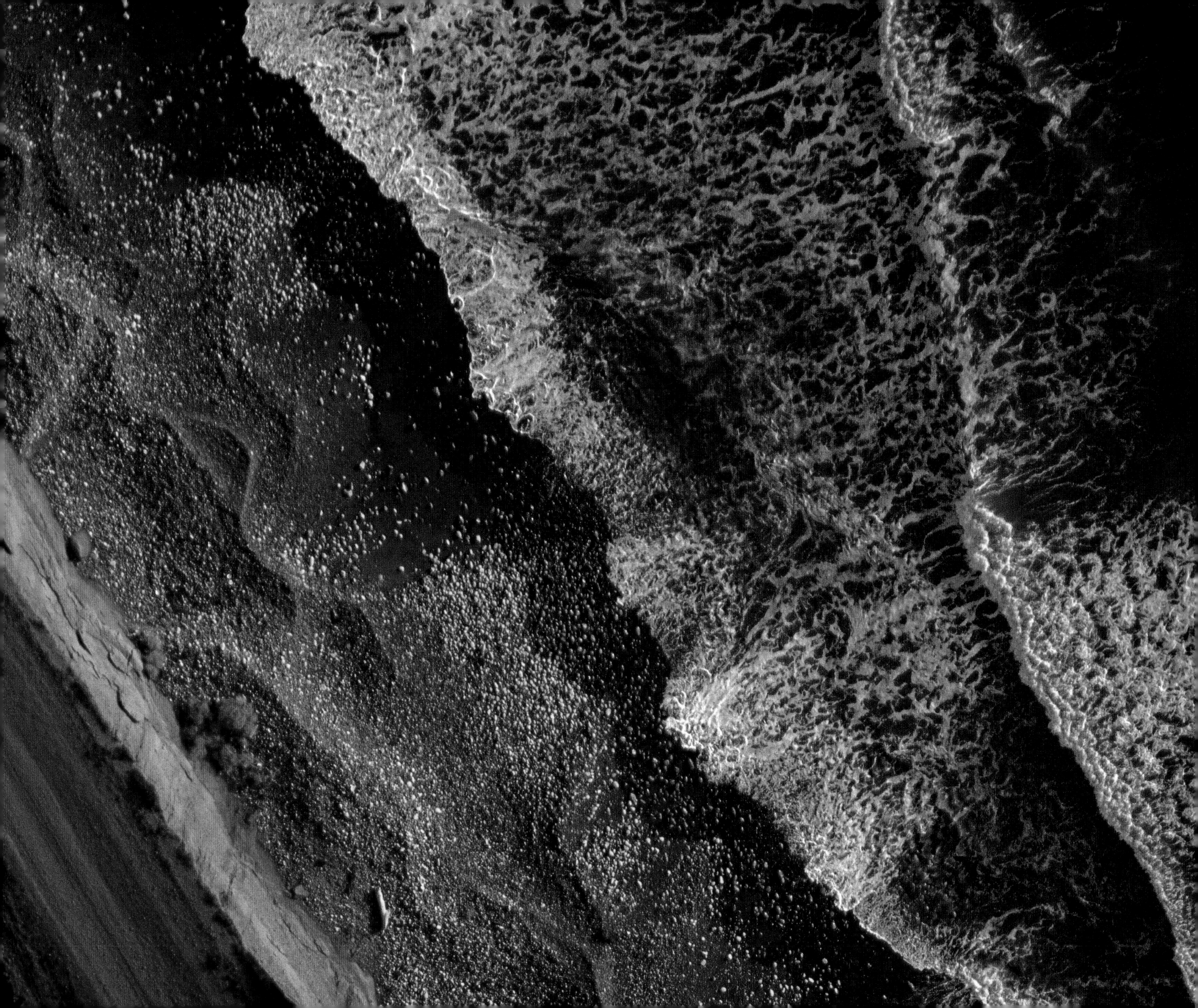

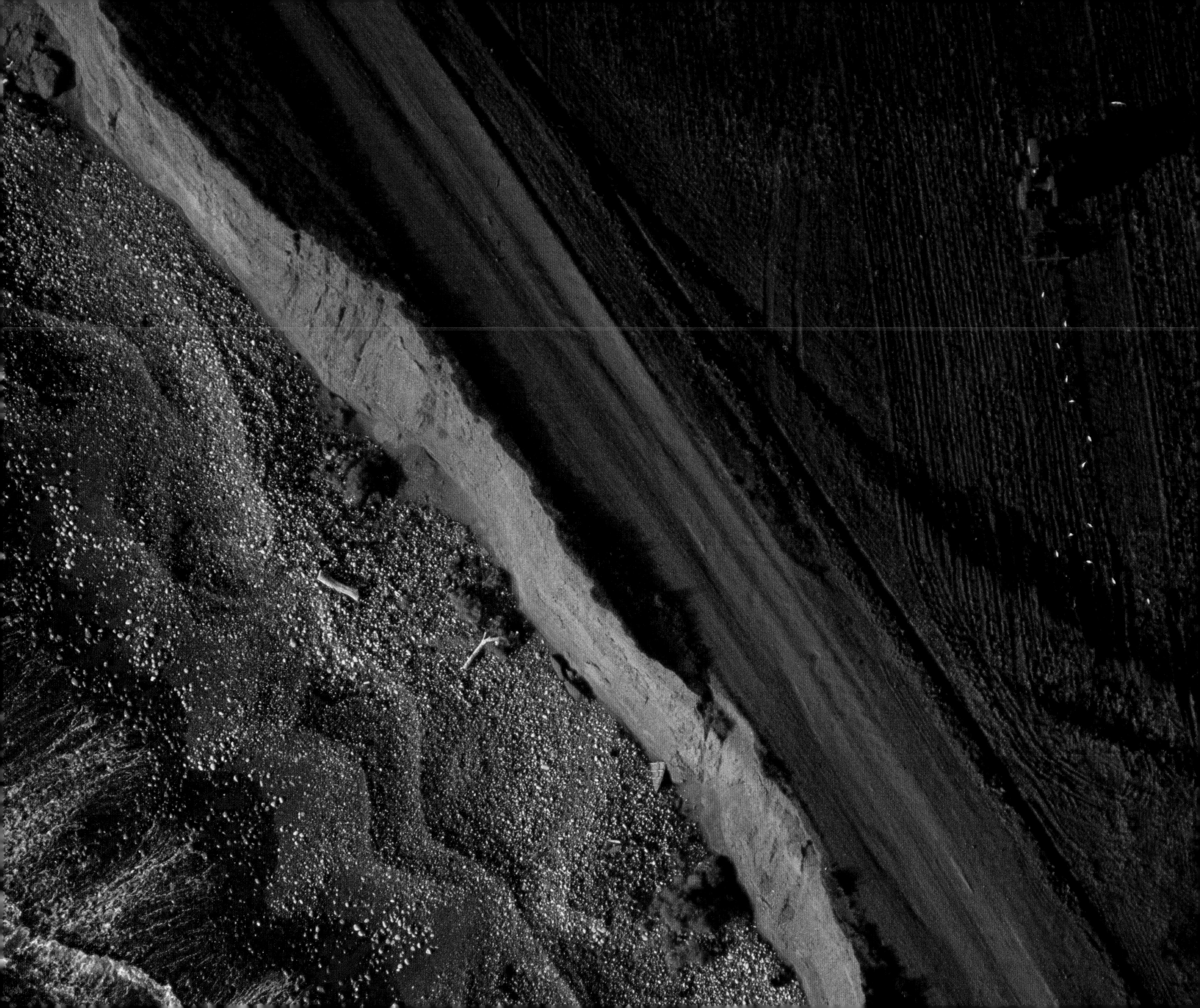

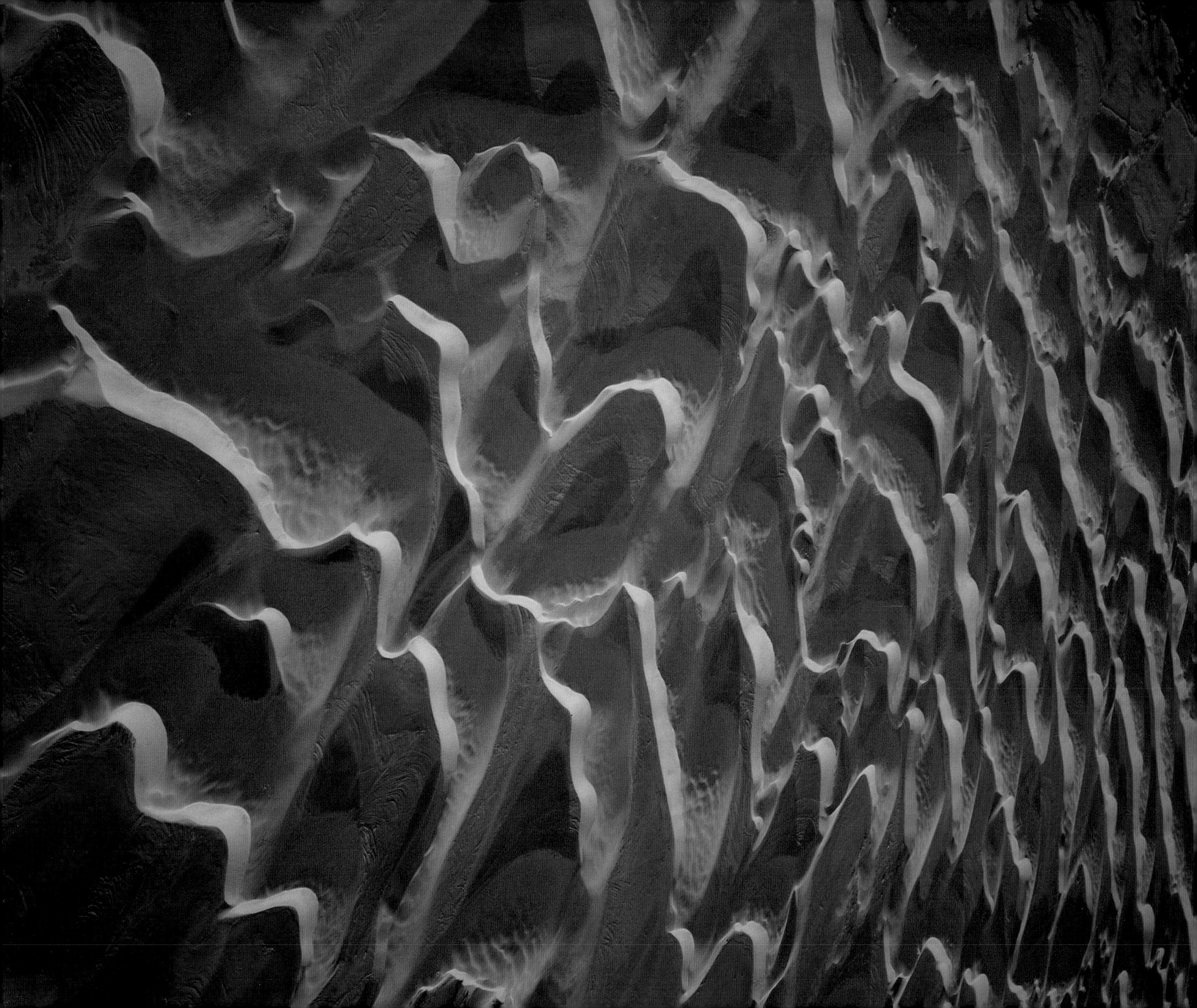

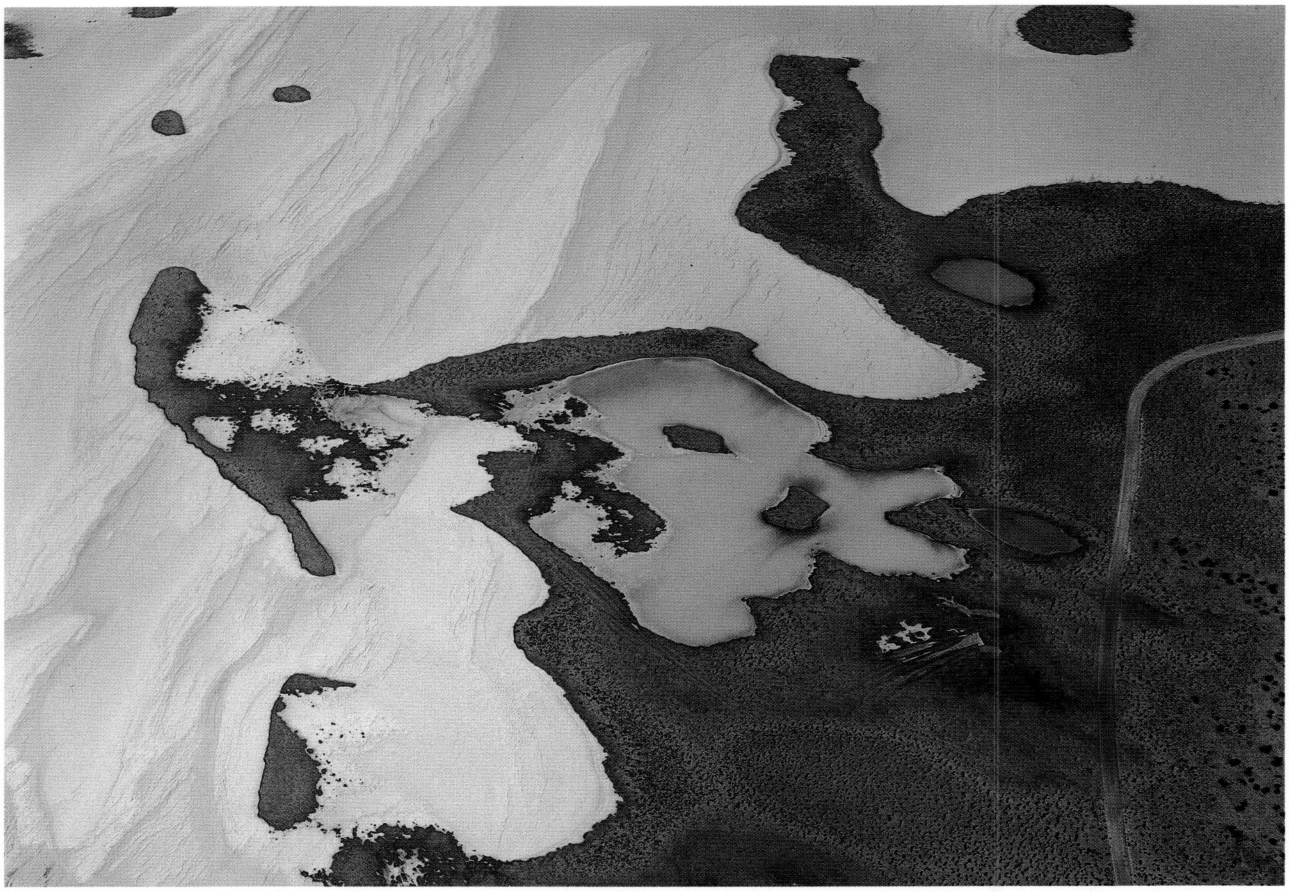

Evaporation patterns on the surface of the salt marshes by Vizcaino Bay.
Tractors scoop up salt deposits in Guerrero Negro.

Wind-shaped sand dunes by Scammon's Lagoon.

Water flow patterns in the marshes of Guerrero Negro.

The delta of the Colorado River.

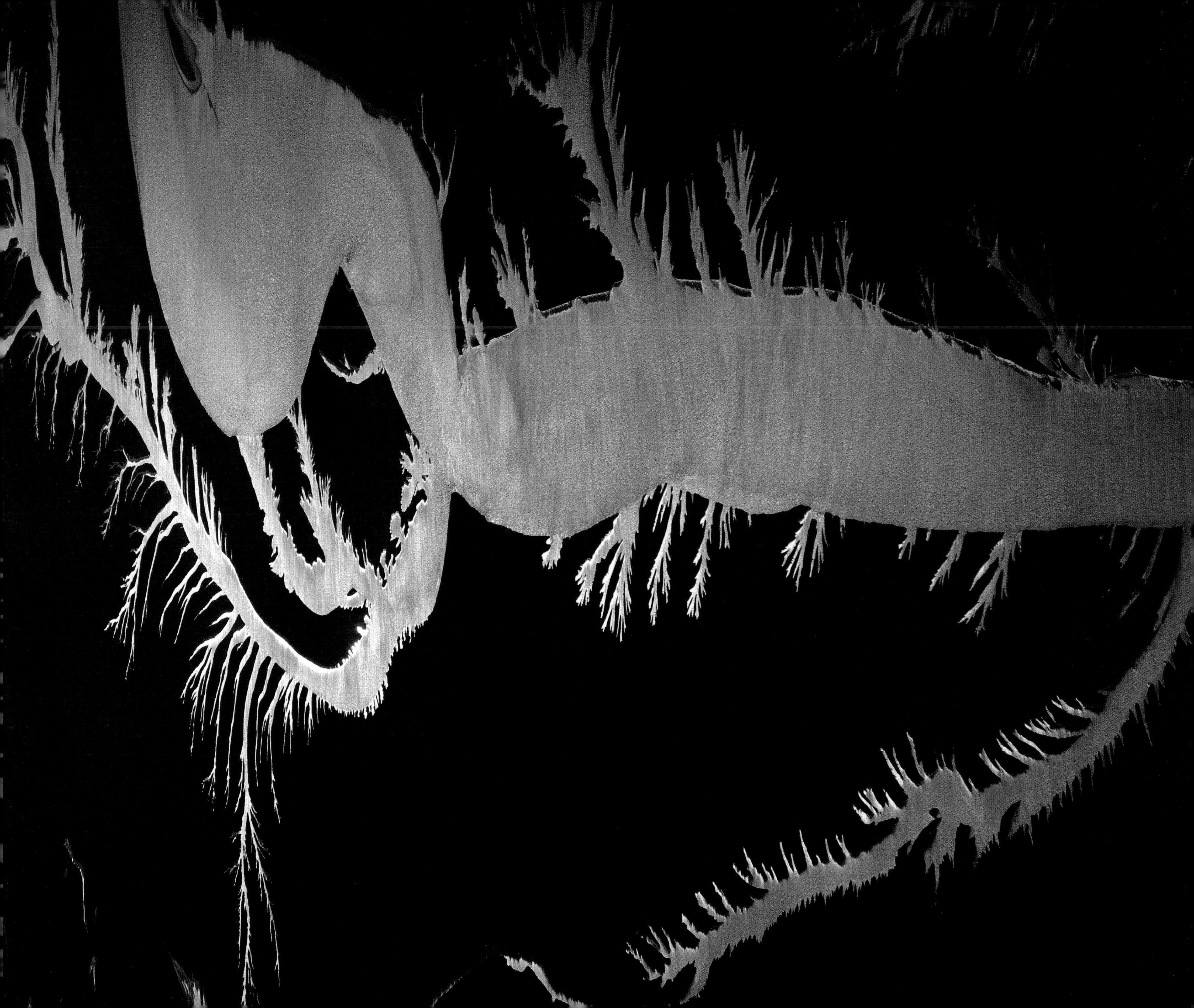

# PHOTOGRAPHY INDEX

**2/3. Mexico's four highest volcanic peaks on a clear winter day.**
In the foreground, the Nevado de Toluca; behind, the Popocatepetl (right) and the Iztaccihuatl (left); on the horizon, the Pico de Orizaba.

**4/5. The Caribbean shoreline of the Yucatan.**

**6/7. The Usumacinta River establishes the border between Mexico and Guatemala.**
Mists form almost daily over the Lacandon rain forest as the sun evaporates the early morning moisture.

**8/9. A natural anchorage, Balandra Bay, shelters a yacht for the night.**

**10. The Tamul waterfalls, at the junction of the Verde and Santa Maria Rivers.**
The El Verde River runs through the Huasteca, a mountainous region of the State of San Luis Potosi. These mountains extend through parts of the States of Hidalgo, Veracruz and Queretaro. Famous for its abundant orchards and coffee and sugar plantations, this area is also home to the *huapangueros*, folk music ensembles whose cheerful falsetto singing is accompanied by fiddle and guitar.

**14. Ruins of Tulum, a fortified city of the ancient Maya on the Caribbean.**
The first mention of Tulum by a Spanish explorer was made by Juan de Grijalva who sailed the coastline in 1518. He wrote that "we saw a town of such a size that the city of Seville could not appear larger or smaller." Facing the sea is the "Castle," a building which most archeologists consider a temple, though there have been recent attempts to prove that its real purpose was as some kind of lighthouse for pre-Columbian shipping.

## THE SOUTHEAST

**24. The Agua Azul falls near the Mayan ruins of Palenque.** The extraordinary blues and greens for which these travertine falls are named are the result of limestone riverbed minerals dissolved in the rivers that flow through the Lacandon rain forest. In areas where the rivers descend abruptly, the precipitation of these minerals form ponds with unnaturally smooth, rounded walls.

**27. High-rise hotels in the resort city of Cancun cast their shadows over the Caribbean.**
Since its initial construction in 1972, the resort has been so successful that the entire coastal strip as far as Tulum is slated for tourist development. Most of the hotels in this view have been built over the last two years. In the 1970s publicists translated the Mayan word *tulum* to mean "pot of gold;" it really means "the place of the snake."

**28. Palenque, a jewel of Classic Mayan architecture.**
Palenque is neither the largest nor the oldest of Mayan sites, but it is one of the most perfectly balanced ceremonial centers ever built by a pre-Columbian civilization. The pyramid set against the hillside is perhaps the only one in Mexico to have been used not only as a place of worship, but also as a tomb, as in ancient Egypt.

**29. Pine and oak woods encircle the lakes of Montebello, Chiapas.** Close to the border of Guatemala, these lakes are famous for the intense hues of their waters. Curiously, no reference is made to this phenomenon in the name; Montebello is Spanish for "beautiful mountain."

**30. A fishing camp on the Gulf side of the Yucatan Peninsula.**

**31. A flamingo colony feeds in the shallow lagoon of the Celestun reserve.**
Every November, the flamingo colonies fly along the northern coast of the Yucatan from their winter home in the Celestun Lagoon to Ria Lagartos, some 150 miles to the east. The journey, however, involves only a change of habitat, not of climate, thus deviating from the pattern of other migrating bird species. The strange browns and purples in the water come from a dye secreted by the roots of the mangrove trees.

**32. The solitary ruins of Edzna, Campeche.**
The flat terrain of the Yucatan is interrupted by hillocks covered with trees and scrub. Many of these are archeological sites waiting to be explored. With the vegetation peeled back and fallen stones replaced, Edzna reveals the majesty of Mayan civilization, hinting at other treasures that still lie undiscovered beneath the jungle canopy. Unfortunately, Mexico cannot allocate sufficient funds for the proper exploration of these sites, and unauthorized treasure hunters operating under cover of the jungle are plundering them.

**33. Ruins of an early Franciscan church, Campeche.**
The Franciscans were the first friars to arrive in Mexico, and their order was mainly responsible for the conversion of Indians to Christianity during the sixteenth century. As in many other cases, this site was probably abandoned as a result of outbreaks of plague that decimated the Indian population in Mexico.

**34/35. Mountain ranges in the highlands of Chiapas.**

**36. Early morning mist blankets the remnants of the Lacandon jungle.** The Lacandon jungle is one of the last tropical rain forests remaining in Mexico but is being systematically destroyed, mainly by migrating farmers, who burn the trees to clear the ground. Devoid of the protection provided by the dense jungle vegetation, the soil loses its fertility and in a few years is suitable only for raising cattle. The loss is irreversible: it is impossible for the forest to regain its original diversity.

**37a. Shoal patterns in the Laguna de Terminos, Campeche.**
The Laguna de Terminos is among the ten largest coastal lagoons in the world.

**37b. Fishing launches cross the sandbanks off Isla Mujeres.**
As the sand dunes in a desert are changed by the wind, the sands visible below the surface of the water are constantly shaped by the sea currents. Within a week, this particular view would be completely different.

**38. The fissured slopes of El Chichonal, a newly active volcano in Chiapas.**
The *chichon* is a dwarf palm only seven feet in height and indigenous to the states of Chiapas and Tabasco. The slopes of the volcano were covered by beautiful palm groves which were destroyed by an eruption in March, 1982. Tons of fine ash spewed into the upper atmosphere which, together with the occurrence of "El Niño," a periodic water current phenomenon in the Pacific Ocean, caused worldwide weather disturbances.

**39. El Castillo, the pyramid dedicated to the serpent god Kukulcan at Chichen-Itza.**
Every equinox at sunrise, the shadow cast by one of the staircases upon the surface of this pyramid is said to resemble the profile of a descending serpent, a spectacle which draws large numbers of tourists. In the early part of this century the building was heavily restored by archeologists, and the famous shadow effect may owe more to the influence of modern stage effects than to the original intentions of the Mayan priesthood.

**40. The temples of Yaxchilan emerge from the Lacandon rain forest.**
A Mayan city built inside a bend of the Usumacinta River, Yaxchilan was discovered in 1888 by the Europeans Alfred Maudslay and Robert Muller, but was barely explored until the early 1970s. The city was raised above the level of the river upon a gigantic platform, large enough for small airplanes to land on. Every year, groups of Lacandon Indians trek through the jungle to make offerings to the ancient gods of Yaxchilan.

**41. The hacienda of Blancaflor, Yucatan.**
Sisal fiber in the Yucatan and coffee in Chiapas brought enormous profits

to landowners during the last decades of the nineteenth century, owing to increasing demand for these products in Europe and the United States. The *hacendados* were constantly in need of cheap labor. There even exist records of a plantation owner in Chiapas who looked as far as the Gilbert Islands in Polynesia, while another in the Yucatan turned to Korea to hire field hands.

**42. Evening thunderstorm bearing down on Isla del Carmen, Campeche.**
The late summer tropical storms along Mexico's coasts are known as hurricanes. The name is derived from a Caribbean Indian language. *Hurakan* was adopted by the early Spanish explorers of the sixteenth century and means "wind of great speed and force."

**43. The Tzotzil Indian town of San Andres Larrainzar, Chiapas.**
Each Tzotzil pueblo has its own particular style of woven costume, recognizable by the combinations of colors in the thread. However, the motifs and patterns of these weavings remain very similar from one place to the other and are rich in symbols related to fertility and the natural cycle of life and death. Some of these patterns may also be found in the garments of pre-Columbian Mayan statuettes.

**44/45. The great Mayan ceremonial center of Uxmal.**
Founded around 400 A.D., Uxmal dominated northeastern Yucatan for three hundred years. Unique to this site are the pyramid with rounded corners and the low-slung buildings of the courtyard. The delicacy of relief patterns on the facades led to the supposition that these buildings had been reserved for an order of priestesses, and the name "Courtyard of the Nuns," coined by the conquistadors, survives to this day.

# THE GULF COAST

**46. The San Pedro y San Pablo River winds across the plain of Tabasco.**
The San Pedro y San Pablo and the Palizadas Rivers branch off the Usamacinta River in the State of Tabasco. The State lies at the southernmost end of the Gulf Coast and receives by far the greatest amount of rainfall in Mexico. If it were to rain as much in the Mississippi basin, the Mississippi River would carry three times its present volume of water.

**49. The sun sets behind a petrochemical refinery at La Cangrejera, Veracruz.**
Owing to extensive investments in petrochemical installations during the oil boom years of the 1970s, Mexico was able to quadruple its output of petrochemical products in less than a decade. Between 1977 and 1987, however, the output of primary oil products, for example gasoline and natural gas, increased by only a third. The Cangrejera complex includes 21 separate petrochemical plants and is the fourth largest in the world.

**50. Primavera trees in full bloom on the coastal plain, Veracruz.**

**51. El Salto waterfall in the Huasteca region, San Luis Potosi.**
The first hydroelectric power plants in Mexico were built along the Gulf Coast by British entrepreneurs, to take advantage of the many waterfalls in the region. Such is the case of El Salto, where most of the water volume is now channeled through enormous pipes down a mountain slope and into the turbines.

**52/53. Early morning clouds surround the cone of the Pico de Orizaba.**
Rising to 18,265 ft., the Pico de Orizaba is Mexico's highest mountain peak. Its great height may explain why pre-Columbian Indians called it the Citlaltepetl, or "Mountain of the Star." Visible far out to sea, the volcano served as a beacon for ships navigating the Gulf during the early days of the Spanish colonies.

**54a. A Pemex oil rig 40 miles into the Sound of Campeche.**
Despite budget cuts and slackening oil prices, Mexico's state-owned oil company has gone ahead with most of its exploratory drilling projects, particularly in the Sound of Campeche, the most promising field so far surveyed in Mexico. National proven reserves are presently estimated at around 69,000 million barrels.

**54b. Veracruz, Mexico's oldest and busiest Gulf port.**
Shipyards, drydocks and quays service the shipping industry while the atmosphere surrounding the central square makes the port a favorite for visiting sailors. The town band, wandering harp and guitar trios, and the clatter of innumerable domino games fill the warm evening with an unending cacophony. "Veracruzanos" have gained a reputation for gaiety; as James Norman wrote, "the city has no architectural wonders—its art is simply the art of living."

**55. Petroleum tanker moorings in the Coatzacoalcos River, Veracruz.**

**56. An example of Mexican naive art, Cupilco, Tabasco.**
The relief on the facade of this church is a celebration of the legend of Guadalupe and depicts in clear and picturesque detail the moment when the Virgin's likeness was miraculously printed upon the cloak of the poor shepherd Juan Diego. To let the townspeople know that the miracle took place in the drier highlands, the artist was careful to place the typical cactus behind Juan Diego. Cacti are rarely found in the humid jungles of Tabasco.

**57. Porticos and balustrades line the streets of Tlacotalpan, Veracruz.**
Every February 2 the revered Virgin of the Candelaria is serenaded by the fishermen of Tlacotalpan. Surrounded by hundreds of skiffs, the barge carrying her image is promenaded up and down the Papaloapan River to the sound of harps and guitars.

**58. The foothills of the Tuxtla volcanos by Playa Escondida, Veracruz.**
The Sierra de los Tuxtla is a volcanic outcrop which for some 50 miles separates the coastal plain from the Gulf. The sight of volcanic cliffs covered by tropical vegetation is more common to Hawaii and certainly unique on the North Atlantic seaboard. Magicians and soothsayers abound among the inhabitants of this area, combining the ancient practices of Olmec religion with African beliefs brought by the slaves who worked the sugar cane fields in Colonial times.

**59. The Miguel Aleman Reservoir in the State of Oaxaca.**
The building of the Aleman Dam transformed the hilly terrain of the Sierra Mazateca into an archipelago of a thousand islands, some of which assumed the most fantastic shapes. Mexico's juiciest and sweetest pineapples are harvested in this region.

# THE CENTRAL PLATEAU

**60. The Paricutin cinder cone, recent proof of Mexico's volcanic geography.**
This is the youngest of more than three hundred volcanos strung along the Neovolcanic Range, which crosses Mexico from the Gulf to the Pacific along the nineteenth parallel and is nearly 550 miles long. Eight of the ten highest mountains in the country appear in this range and they are all volcanos. From a botanical point of view, it marks the boundary between the temperate and the tropical zones.

**63. Early morning mist rises from a hillside near Apan, Hidalgo.**
Despite abundant woodlands and a rich variety of native tree species, the amount of timber obtained in Mexico is relatively low. The difficulties posed by mountainous terrain and inefficient forestry techniques are just two reasons for this lack of productivity. The entire Mexican timber and wood industry amounts to barely 0.5% of the gross national product. Nonetheless, the destruction of forests at present rates may leave Mexico without wood-

lands in less than thirty years. It is clear that the ecological importance of Mexican woods far outstrips the economical benefits of their exploitation.

**64. A crater provides a ready-made wall for a farmer's field.**
Mexico covers an area larger than Spain, France, Portugal, Italy, Germany and Great Britain put together, but only a ninth of the territory may be farmed. Of this land, slightly more than 80% is cultivated annually. Even the cones of ancient volcanos are put under the plow, due to their fertile soil.

**65. Mexico's oldest bullring during the spring fair of San Marcos, Aguascalientes.**
Bullfighting in Mexico dates from the very first days of Spanish dominion. An early bullfighter was Hernan Cortes, captain of the conquistadors. In 1552, one of his cousins founded the cattle ranch of San Mateo Atenco, 60 miles from Mexico City. It is the world's oldest *ganaderia*, or ranch, specializing in the breeding of bulls for bullfights.

**66. Agricultural terracing cut into the hills of the Sierra de Tentzo, Puebla.**
Although it is essential for soil conservation on hillsides, agricultural terracing is an uncommon sight in Mexico. Traditionally, the *campesinos* clear the mountain slopes for subsistence farming, rendering the soil unsuitable for agriculture within a few years. The need to increase corn yields to feed a rapidly expanding population is revolutionizing the old methods of farming.

**67. Ripening wheat fields near Apan, Hidalgo.**
In times of the Colony, these fields were mostly used for cattle breeding, but by the end of the nineteenth century, they were covered with vast agave plantations. The railroad enabled the landowners to exploit the lucrative market of nearby Mexico City by selling pulque, a fermentation of agave sap. Today, more beer is drunk than pulque so the fields are given over to the cultivation of wheat and barley.

**68/69. Uneven terrain forced the abandonment of the traditional street grids in Taxco (left) and Guanajuato (right).**
The similarities between Taxco and Guanajuato go no further than their crooked streets and their common origin as mining camps. A small town dominated by the magnificent church of Santa Prisca, Taxco remains dependent on silver for its economic survival. Guanajuato has developed into a cosmopolitan city, the capital of its province since the eighteenth century. Today it is seat of a local university and every fall hosts Mexico's most prestigious arts festival.

**70/71. The Pyramids of the Moon (above) and the Sun (right), Teotihuacan.**
The Pyramid of the Sun is only half as tall as the Pyramid of Cheops in Egypt, although its base is almost the same size. The pyramid was made of adobe bricks covered with a layer of stones and red stucco. It was built on a natural cave, which ends in a grotto, shaped like a four-petaled flower, at the pyramid's center. The pyramids of Teotihuacan were not built as tombs for their kings, but as religious centers.
The Pyramid of the Moon and its plaza lies at the end of the Avenue of the Dead, a two-and-a-half mile long axis that served as the backbone of the whole city. At its peak, the city covered some 61 square miles, a surface larger than that of imperial Rome. Present day visitors have access only to one-fiftieth of that area, but are nonetheless overwhelmed by the sheer size of the site.

**72. *Charro* traditions were founded in the stockraising ranches of Jalisco.**
In the sixteenth century, Spanish ranchers left their stock free to graze, but animals frequently invaded and damaged the cornfields of Indian communities, resulting in constant tension between the natives and the Spaniards. The invention of the *charro* saddle, essential for the herding of cattle from horseback, is attributed to Don Luis de Velasco, second Viceroy of Mexico.

**73a. Strip field patterns surround a Puebla village.**
This view is reminiscent of European villages of the Middle Ages. However, rural society in Mexico today is more structurally varied, due to the economic and social differences separating its members. Broadly speaking, at least three different groups may be distinguished: Indian *campesinos* devoted to subsistence farming and local crafts, *rancheros* or farmers who may also invest in small businesses of their own, and well-financed *agricultores*, who manage their concerns according to the most advanced modern methods.

**73b. A bend in the Atoyac River, Puebla.**

**74. Erosion patterns in the highlands of Jalisco.**
Mismanagement of land resources in Mexico dates back to the sixteenth century. At that time, great areas of woodland were cut down to provide fuel for the silver smelters and timber for the construction of houses for Spanish settlers.

**75. Fields of African marigolds destined for Day of the Dead graveyard altars.**
Every November 2, Mexicans flock to the graveyards to honor their dead relatives. It is customary to decorate the tombs with marigolds, a photograph of the deceased, and all kinds of food, since it is common belief that the souls are allowed to return to earth on that day. It is not an occasion for mourning, but for fond recollection of times past, heightened by the prospect of sharing with the dead relative his favorite dishes.

**76. The tower and nave of Parangaricutiro church jut from the Paricutin lava beds.**
Every Mexican school child is taught the story of farmer Dionisio Pulido, who one day noticed a wisp of smoke rising from a newly plowed cornfield. It was only a matter of weeks before the Paricutin volcano buried not only Pulido's farm, but the village of San Juan Parangaricutiro beneath layers of lava.

**77. Church in Jolalpan, Puebla.**
A new coat of paint illustrates the importance of church life in Mexico.

**78/79. Water-filled craters of long extinct volcanos on the plains of Puebla.**

**80. A unique arrangement of plazas surrounding the Cathedral of Guadalajara.**
Unlike any other colonial city in Mexico, the center of Guadalajara is composed of a series of squares laid out around the cathedral. Although they give the appearance of careful planning, the squares were opened in different epochs of Guadalajara's history. The cathedral itself took centuries to reach its present form. Its spires were added in the mid-nineteenth century and have achieved national fame through the lyrics of a mariachi song.

**81. The domes and belltowers of Guadalajara silhouetted against the rising sun.**
During colonial times, Guadalajara was less important than other provincial cities in Mexico. Rapid recovery from the revolutionary fighting of the 1910s transformed it into the country's second largest metropolis.

**82. The Hacienda of Chiautla, an architectural curiosity in Puebla.**
In the late nineteenth century, travel to Europe became fashionable and many hacienda owners remodeled their old properties to look like castles. The case of Chiautla is slightly different, in that it was originally built in imitation of a French chateau.

**83. An irrigated plain dotted with *huizache* trees, Puebla.**
The *huizache* is a species of acacia that grows not only in the eastern half of the central plateau, but also in the arid northern regions of Chihuahua, Sonora and Tamaulipas. The flowers produce an oily liquid used to perfume cosmetics and the bark, rich in tannin, may be used to tan leather.

**84. The cupolas of the Royal Chapel in the monastery of San Gabriel, Cholula.**
This building is one of the many architectural oddities created by the friars during the first decades of Spanish dominion. The plan for the cathedral of Patzcuaro, with five naves placed like the fingers of an opened hand, was a similar flight of fancy. The arrival of orthodox architects put an end to such experiments.

**85. Country church, Puebla.**
Around the city of Puebla even the smallest churches are richly tiled. Puebla was specifically founded for those conquistadors who, having won the battle for Mexico, were unwilling to lay down their arms and roamed the countryside in lawless bands. To encourage them to settle down, they were granted many privileges and Puebla soon became the manufacturing center of New Spain, with glass, cloth and ceramics as its main products. The custom of using brightly colored Talavera tiles in the church domes of Puebla spread to almost every corner of Mexico.

**86. Lake Patzcuaro, former site of the Purepecha Indian civilization.**
There is a legend that tells of a tribe who came across the lake of Patzcuaro. A group of them decided to stop and take a bath. The rest feigned agreement

but soon ran off with the clothing and property of the bathers. In a fit of pique, the bathers gave up the language, religion and customs of their ancestors and settled by the lake, thereby giving birth to the Purepecha civilization.

**87. The main square of San Miguel de Allende, shaded by clipped laurel trees.**
An increasing number of tourists are drawn to San Miguel de Allende by its well-preserved colonial architecture. It is therefore ironic that the town should be mostly identified by the church spire, which was recently added to the original colonial structure by a self-taught mason.

**88. Winter snows crown the Nevado de Toluca volcano.**
The road that winds up the mountainside actually leads into the crater of this extinct volcano, the fourth highest in Mexico.

**89. The Sun and Moon Lagoons in the crater of the Nevado de Toluca.**
Clay pots and offerings found by underwater archeological explorations have shown that pre-Columbian Indians, probably the Matlatzinca tribe, held various religious rites beside these lagoons.

# MEXICO CITY

**90. *Trajineras*, or punts, await a busy Sunday morning in the canals of Xochimilco.**
During the second half of the nineteenth century steamboats briefly navigated the canals and lakes that connected Mexico City with Texcoco, Chalco, Xochimilco and many smaller nearby towns. Still, the *trajineras* remained the common transportation for campesinos. The growth of the capital led to the draining of the lakes and the *trajineras* are now limited to ferrying tourists around the remaining canals of Xochimilco, accompanied by snacks and mariachi music.

**93. The Monument to the Independence of Mexico on Reforma Boulevard.**
This monument was erected to celebrate the centennial of the beginning of the war of Independence and is commonly known as "The Angel," because of the winged statue on top. An earthquake in 1957 toppled the gilded bronze from its perch. Jokes were then made about "the angel who was learning to fly." Before the tragic events of 1985, Mexicans tended to be quite casual about earthquakes.

**94. Paseo de la Reforma, once the Mayfair of Mexico City.**
Laid out by the French-imposed emperor, Maximilian I, the boulevard provided a short-cut between the imperial offices and the palace atop Chapultepec Hill. Reforma was later embellished with trees and statues of Mexican heroes, many of whom had fought against Maximilian. Curiously, some thirty years after the Mexicans overthrew Maximilian'sempire, Paris fashion was de rigueur in Mexico, and French-style mansions sprang up along Reforma. Among the office high-rises that now line the boulevard an occasional relic of the belle epoque in Mexico has survived.

**95. Itinerant street market sets up for the day.**

**96/97. The old quarter of Mexico City, built over the ruins of Tenochtitlan.**
Built in the middle of a lake and crossed by a network of canals, sixteenth century Mexico City was described by Miguel de Cervantes as "the Venice of the Indies." Like its Italian counterpart, the city suffered several disastrous floods during colonial times. Worst of all was the flood of 1629, after which Mexico City lay under nearly five feet of water for almost three years. Ironically, the city also suffered badly from the lack of sufficient drinking-water supplies.

**98. A Diego Rivera fountain inspired by pre-Columbian myths.**
A controversial artist and political radical, Rivera devoted much of his remarkable talent to the rescue of Mexico's heritage. The fountain, next to the pumphouse of an aqueduct, represents the Aztec rain deity Tlaloc, whose name stems from the verb *tlalli*, meaning "to lie on the ground." The word *totopamitl*, written in the lower left corner of the fountain, is Nahuatl for "corn stalk."

**99. Environmental sculpture amidst the lava fields of the University of Mexico campus.**
This is the largest in a series of monumental sculptures commissioned by University officials to make use of an unusual environment. A lava crust, up to 35 feet thick, covers some 30 square miles southwest of downtown Mexico City. Most of it was produced by the Xitle volcano that erupted around the beginning of the Christian era.

**100. The Palace of Chapultepec, surrounded by Chapultepec Park.**
This is the main park in Mexico City, and its tradition as a place of recreation goes back to pre-Columbian times, when Aztec emperors used the waters of a spring at the foot of Chapultepec Hill to create an early botanical garden in which to relax and contemplate the natural world. Construction of the palace dates back to the late eighteenth century. It was never occupied by the Spanish viceroys but served instead as an archive, a military school, and home to the ill-fated emperor Maximilian I. Today, it is a museum.

**101. The open-air big cat cages at the zoo in Chapultepec Park.**
This zoo has attained world-wide fame in recent years, thanks to its successes in breeding endangered species, such as the giant panda bear.

**102. Modern housing blocks encircle the Aztec pyramid and colonial church in Tlatelolco.**
At the time of the conquest, Tlatelolco was the commercial hub of the Valley of Mexico. Its marketplace left a deep impression on the Spanish soldiers because of the "great quantities of merchandise and the evidence of order and careful arrangement to be observed in everything." In the sixteenth century, Franciscan friars established a school in Tlatelolco devoted solely to the education of Indian children with noble ancestry. One of its alumni went on to study law in the University of Salamanca in Spain, an unusual event for the times.

**103. The Palace of Fine Arts, on the edge of the Alameda Park.**
This grandiose turn-of-the-century opera house was one of several public buildings financed by President Diaz's administration as proof of the advent of modern progress in Mexico. It was outfitted with the latest in stage gadgetry, including a movie projection booth.

**104/105. The Cathedral of the Virgin and the National Palace on the Zocalo square.**
Although the foundations of the Cathedral were laid four hundred years ago, it is still the largest Catholic building in Latin America and required almost two hundred years to complete. The National Palace has been the seat of political power ever since colonial times. It was built upon the ruins of the palaces of the last Aztec emperors. Officially entitled "Constitution Plaza," the main square of the city is known to every Mexican as the "Zocalo," Spanish for plinth or pedestal. In the 1840s, the government of General Santa Anna decided to erect a monument on the square. Santa Anna was soon deposed, with only the plinth completed; it remained in the square for several decades until a later government demolished it. By then the populace had adopted the name "Zocalo" for the square itself.

**106. December 12th festivities at the shrine of Guadalupe.**
Pilgrims form squares around the Concheros, Indian groups dressed in exotic costumes who honor the Virgin of Guadalupe by dancing in the esplanade of the Basilica. Dancing in pre-Columbian Mexico had a ritual purpose and in the Conchero dances there are still undercurrents of these ancient ceremonies beneath the gloss of Christianity.

**107. Sculpture by Alexander Calder in the esplanade of the Azteca Stadium.**

# THE PACIFIC COAST

**108. Cliffs and waves outlined by the early morning sunlight, Michoacan.**

**111. Small boats and bathers crowd the waters along Caleta Beach, Acapulco.**
Visitors during the 1930s and 1940s were first attracted to Acapulco by the spectacular landscape of the Bay of Santa Lucia. Vacation houses were built

on the cliffs overlooking the sea. In the 1950s, the sheltered beaches of Caleta and Caletilla became fashionable for sunbathing and swimming, but the construction of luxury hotels further along the bay returned these beaches to the local folk.

**112. Full moon rising over Acapulco and the Bay of Santa Lucia.**
In the space of a few decades Acapulco has grown from an insignificant fishing port into a modern city with close to one million inhabitants. In the foreground is La Roqueta, an island at the mouth of the bay which only the lack of drinking water has kept free of development.

**113. The Fort of San Diego watching over a cruise ship in Acapulco.**
The Fort of San Diego was built in 1776 on the site of an earlier fortification. The influence of Vauban, the French military engineer, is clearly visible in its pentagonal design with bastions at each corner. The enduring presence of this fortress, now a museum, reminds the casual visitor that Acapulco has a history prior to the era of high-rise hotels and condos.

**114a. Fishing trawler stranded on the sands of Barra de Navidad, Jalisco.**

**114b. Heavy waves break on the exposed rocks of the Jalisco coastline.**
The surface of the earth is divided into huge segments, known as plates, which are in constant motion. Two of these, the Cocus and the North American Plates, push against one another along the Mexican Pacific coast, moving at a speed of several inches every year. The rocky coastline from Jalisco to the Isthmus of Tehuantepec is largely the result of the pressure generated by these two plates, which is also the cause of 35 major earthquakes that have shaken Mexico during this century.

**115. The Pitutina lighthouse overlooking Campos Cove, Michoacan.**

**116. The Valley of Oaxaca on a clear afternoon before the summer rains.**
The harvests in almost three quarters of the arable land in Mexico depend on a rainy season that has never been regular or easy to predict, with drought a constant threat. It is easy to understand why the rain deities were essential to pre-Columbian mythology.

**117. The active Volcan de Fuego and the extinct Nevado de Colima, Jalisco.**
The Volcan de Fuego is not only one of Mexico's highest peaks, but its most active volcano. This activity is mostly restricted to clouds of fumes and occasional rumblings. However, vulcanologists estimate that a major eruption should occur in the next few decades.

**118/119. The acropolis of Monte Alban overlooking the Valley of Oaxaca.**
Monte Alban was founded around 600 B.C. by the Zapotec Indians, on a mountain rising 4,000 feet above the surrounding valleys. It is estimated that up to 25,000 inhabitants lived on the slopes leading to the ceremonial center of the city. Among the most enduring of the pre-Columbian civilizations, the Zapotecs left at least 200 other archeological sites in the vicinity of Monte Alban.

**120. A country churchyard bougainvilla in the Valley of Oaxaca.**
Church forecourts which serve as graveyards are common all over the world. However in Mexico the forecourts tend to be disproportionately large. In the early days of Spanish dominion, walled open spaces with stone crosses at their center served to convert the Indians to Christianity and to perform baptisms and masses. In time, the church would be built, usually on the eastern edge of the square. This basic layout remained long after the evangelists had completed their task.

**121. Fields of hibiscus in flower along the coast of Guerrero.**
A hot climate has inspired the inhabitants of Guerrero to invent a variety of refreshments with which to quench their thirst. Water flavored with hibiscus flowers is a particular favorite.

**122. Palms and red earth characterize the Tierra Caliente of Oaxaca.**
The Chatino Indians of Oaxaca are descended from the Zapotecs who built Monte Alban, one of Mexico's most spectacular ceremonial centers. They have managed to maintain a way of life that is beyond European influence.

**123. Sandbanks at a river mouth on the Oaxaca coastline.**
This photograph was taken near the Isthmus of Tehuantepec, where Mexico's only matriarchy operates.

**124a. Oceanside twelfth hole on the Las Hadas golf course, Manzanillo.**

**124b. Yacht flying a spinnaker off the coast of Mazatlan.**

**125. Moorish inspiration is evident in the resort village of Las Hadas, Manzanillo.**

**126. The coastal resort of Puerto Vallarta.**
Most of the resorts along the Pacific coast have evolved from towns that were founded before the eighteenth century. Although the arrival of tourism transformed Acapulco, the old quarters in Mazatlan and Puerto Vallarta have kept their old-world charm. In Mazatlan the city grew along the coast, away from downtown. Puerto Vallarta, on the other hand, has grown around the original town, providing a traditional center to a new city.

**127. Seaside villa on the cliffs of Careyes, Jalisco.**
In the construction of luxury seaside villas, modern Mexican architects have discovered the value of thatched roofs, adobe walls and other indigenous building techniques as an alternative to air conditioning. The use of rustic materials has also yielded a distinctive architectural style.

**128a. Mexcaltitan, perhaps the original island home of the Aztecs.**
According to legend, the Aztec tribe migrated as pilgrims in search of the promised land from their primal home in Aztlan to the Valley of Mexico where they founded Mexico-Tenochtitlan. Historians are not sure of the exact location of Aztlan but there are several similarities between the fishing village of Mexcaltitan and descriptions of ancient Mexico City. Both have names connected to the word *mextli*, or moon, both are sited in the middle of lagoons, and the layout of contemporary Mexcaltitan bears a remarkable resemblance to that of Mexico-Tenochtitlan.

**128b. Cows travel a watery path on their way home to Mexcaltitan.**

**129. Mangrove swamps near San Blas, Nayarit.**
Only in recent years have natural scientists begun to understand the importance of swamps in the earth's life sustaining cycles. Some studies have linked the productivity of marine fisheries to the cleansing processes performed by mangroves and other water plants. In Mexico, however, swamps continue to be drained and turned over to grazing cattle. The long-term consequences on the environment of this practice are unknown.

**130. The traditional fishing town of Puerto Escondido, Oaxaca.**
Puerto Escondido is one of the few Pacific tourist destinations which has retained the flavor of a traditional fishing town in spite of the disruptive appearance of hotels, airports and beachwear boutiques. Local folk also boast that these are the clearest waters on the Pacific coast, almost as transparent as those of the Caribbean.

**131. The port and tourist resort of Mazatlan.**
The Mexican government has designated the tourist industry as a major factor in the economic growth of the country. Due to its northern location and its temperate waters, Mazatlan has enjoyed increasing popularity among Americans and Canadians.

## THE NORTHEAST

**132. Real de Catorce, ghost town, in the "Silver Belly" hills.**
It was not until the mid-eighteenth century that the silver veins of Real de Catorce were discovered, but it soon became one of Mexico's most important mining towns. Output reached a peak in 1803, when the mines produced three and a half million pesos worth of silver bullion. Between 1863 and 1869 the Catorce Mint coined another six million pesos, but production then decreased until flooding closed the shafts during the Mexican Revolution.

**135. The mouth of the Rio Grande River on the Gulf of Mexico.**
For over two hundred years, teams of explorers "discovered" the river at

separate points along its course, which resulted in a confusing set of names, most of them long forgotten: River of our Lady, Tigurex, Guadalquivir, River of the North, San Buenaventura, Muddy River, etc. With its headwaters in the San Juan Mountains of Colorado, the Rio Grande is one of the longest rivers on the American continent, so it is appropriate its eventual name should mean "big." Rio Bravo, the other surviving name, means "fierce river" and was given by a group of Spanish explorers who narrowly escaped drowning in one of its violent floods.

**136. Saddle Mountain dominates the cityscape of Monterrey.**
Monterrey is famous throughout Mexico for an uninviting climate, where extreme winter is followed by extreme summer almost without transition. Summer droughts are followed by the violent rains of early fall. When hurricanes sweep in from the Gulf Coast, the broad Santa Catarina riverbed, visible to the right of the photograph, becomes a fierce torrent that vanishes as suddenly as it appeared.

**137. A** *campesino* village on the plains of Zacatecas.
Many acres of once arid plains in northern Mexico have been transformed into productive farmland through irrigation. The soil is unusually fertile and the pronounced extremes in temperature between day and night effectively check the spread of pests.

**138. La Quemada, northern outpost of pre-Columbian culture in Zacatecas.**
Dominating the valley of Malpaso, La Quemada protected trade routes from the marauding Chichimeca tribes, firstly for the Teotihuacans who built the outpost around 500 A.D., and for the Aztecs 950 years later. Historians have also suggested that La Quemada was actually the site of Chicomoztoc, a place mentioned in Aztec chronicles where the tribe rested for several years before proceeding southward on their trek to the Valley of Mexico.

**139. The head of the Eastern Sierra Madre, Nuevo Leon.**
The sight of these sheer walls looming over the invading U.S. Army of 1846 fired the imagination of a young lieutenant who wrote home: "Their castellated appearance is most beautiful and reminds you of many descriptions in romance. You have only to let the imagination loose, and these fairy halls, castles and towers are thronged with actors of former ages."

**140. Soccer field squeezed between factory walls in Monterrey.**
Soccer and baseball were first played in Mexico around the turn of the century, but live TV broadcasting of soccer matches during the 1950s contributed substantially to football's rise in popularity. However, baseball still boasts of strongholds along the Gulf Coast and in the northwestern states of Sinaloa and Sonora, where Fernando Valenzuela first played.

**141. The Mexican fondness for color is illustrated in the colonial mining town of Fresnillo, Zacatecas.**

**142. Sandstone cliffs in the Sierra del Carmen, Coahuila.**
Beyond the mountains of the Sierra del Carmen, the Rio Grande runs along the bottom of a canyon 60 miles long and almost 2,000 feet deep. The opposite side of the canyon falls within the Big Bend National Park. Conservationists would like to see an equivalent park in Mexico to preserve the area's dwindling wildlife.

**143. The evening sky of Zacatecas reflected in a country pond.**

**144/145. The mining city of Zacatecas clustered around a Baroque cathedral.**
Within a year of the discovery of silver in Zacatecas, 34 mining companies were exploiting some of the richest seams in the world. Although mining is still important to the Zacatecan economy, the city-scape of narrow alleys winding between vintage colonial houses and churches of pink and yellow sandstone has not been obscured by industrial development.

**146. Traditional shrimp boats in the Laguna Madre.**

**147. A one hundred mile sand bar divides the Laguna Madre from the Gulf of Mexico.**
The sand bar continues north of the mouth of the Rio Grande and almost reaches the port of Galveston, Texas.

# THE NORTHWEST

**148. The Barranca del Cobre canyon in Chihuahua.**
At its deepest point, the canyon drops more than 4,000 feet into the Urique River. Tropical plants flourish in the canyon bottom, while oak and pine woods cover the rim. Deposits of silver, copper, lead and zinc have been surveyed here, but these will not be exploited, as the area has been declared a national park.

**151. A stream brings life to the salt flats of Altata Bay, Sinaloa.**

**152. Wheat fields harvested by the Menonite farm colonies of Chihuahua.**
Menonites settled the plains of Chihuahua after President Obregon signed a special bill of rights granting them an economic regime of their choice and absolute control over their community schools. This enabled the sect to maintain a lifestyle unrelated to the rest of Mexico. The Menonites have established other communities in the states of Durango, Campeche and Guanajuato, and some have migrated to Belize and Bolivia.

**153. Hacienda dominated by its chapel on the plains of Chihuahua.**
Politics and economy in Chihuahua during the second half of the nineteenth century were controled by local feudal relationships, sometimes with the complicity and sometimes in spite of President Porfirio Diaz. Frustrated with the stifling political and economic situation in their home state, the Chihuahuans took up arms against both Diaz and the hacienda-owning families to begin the Mexican Revolution. General Pascual Orozco, a Chihuahuan, led the rebels to victory in the battle of Ciudad Juarez, which sealed the fate of the aging dictator.

**154/155. Rocas de Lumbre, or Rocks of Fire, Chihuahua.**

**156. The headwaters of the Conchos River, Chihuahua.**
The Conchos drains a sizable area of the eastern watershed of the Chihuahuan mountain ranges and provides the Rio Grande with more than half of its water volume.

**157. Autumn colors in the birch woods of Chihuahua.**
The sight of silver birches growing this far south is uncommon. Mexico is a land of diverse climates, due to the combination of a geographical location along the Tropic of Cancer and its largely mountainous terrain. This climatic diversity has resulted in unusually varied plant life. Botanists do not know the exact number of different species growing in Mexico, but they are more numerous than in the Soviet Union which is eleven times bigger in territory.

**158. Modern highrises have changed the cityscape of old Chihuahua.**

**159. The clay remains of Casas Grandes, ancient town of the Chihuahuan Desert.**
Casas Grandes, or Big Houses, was the southernmost outpost of the Pueblo Indian cultures of Arizona and New Mexico. It is archeologically unique in being the only site in Mexico where the dwellings of common folk have survived together with their ceremonial buildings. A ritual ball court has been unearthed and proves that the religious practices of the inhabitants of Casas Grandes were influenced by the cultures of central Mexico.

**160. Tarahumara Indian church in the canyon region of Chihuahua.**
Like other Mexican Indians, the Tarahumarans practise Catholicism intermingled with older tribal beliefs. They have also fiercely resisted assimilation into modern society. It is likely that within this church the ancient gods of the moon and the sun will occupy the same altar as the figure of Christ.

**161a. A rural train bound for Ciudad Juarez crosses the Chihuahuan plains.**
Concessions to build a railway from El Paso to Topolobampo on the Pacific Ocean were once eagerly sought by American entrepreneurs, primarily because Topolobampo is a full 300 miles closer to Saint Louis, Missouri, than Saint Louis is to San Francisco Bay. However, the 250 mile stretch across the Sierra Madre required the building of 39 bridges and 71 tunnels. At one place along this stretch, a single grade zigzags down the same mountainside from the line summit at 7,870 feet to the Chinipas River at 650 feet above sea level.

**161b. Pelicans on the Abelardo Rodriguez Reservoir, Hermosillo, Sonora.**
In an amusing reversal of roles, flying humans gaze down on sedentary pelicans who have discovered an evening roost just below the surface of the dam. The birds were quite unconcerned by the aircraft circling above them, enjoying no doubt their parody of earthbound life and two of its major preoccupations: gossiping and standing in line.

**162. Fishing boats moored to a central buoy in the harbor of Puerto Peñasco, Sonora.**
Puerto Peñasco is a major shrimp port along the Sea of Cortes. Shrimp catches have declined in recent years, but it is not clear whether the shrimp beds are being overexploited or if more complicated environmental factors are involved. As the exportation of shrimp provides the Northwest with valuable income, the solution may lie in increasing the number of shrimp farms in the area.

**163. The Infiernillo Straits separate Isla Tiburon from the Sonora coast.**
Isla Tiburon, or Shark Island, is inhabited by the Seri Indians, one of the last northwestern tribes to remain on the fringes of mestizo Mexico. This is largely due to their physical separation from the mainland by a treacherous stretch of water, known as the Straits of Hell.

**164. An extinct volcano in the Cerro del Pinacate National Park, Sonora.**
Pinacate derives from the Aztec name for a small beetle which secretes a foul-smelling liquid to fend off attackers. This forbidding region is home to several unique species of animals, including a subspecies of pinacate. There are over 600 volcanic craters in the Park, a feature NASA engineers took advantage of to test the moon buggy for the Apollo program.

**165. Volcanic outcrops of the Altar Desert blaze in the early morning sun.**

**166. The Basaseachic Waterfall in the mountains of Chihuahua.**
At 1,020 feet, this is Mexico's highest waterfall, now designated a national park.

**167. The Sierra del Nido rises abruptly from the Chihuahuan prairie.**

## BAJA CALIFORNIA

**168. Sandbanks in Balandra Bay, Baja California Sur.**
About eight miles due north of the city of La Paz, visitors and townspeople alike make their way to Balandra Bay, attracted by the warm shallow waters and sand as fine and white as talcum powder. The varying colors in the water depend on the rise and fall of the subaquatic sandbanks.

**171. Sand and vegetation meet at Santa Maria Bay.**
The dark area in the foreground and the tiny specks close to the background mountain range are mangrove swamps. The winding canal is not a river stream, though it may seem so, but only an estuary. In the lower left corner, the quiet waters of Magdalena Bay contrast with the heavy surf of the Pacific Ocean on Santa Maria Bay.

**172. Isla Espiritu Santo, Baja California Sur.**
The Baja California peninsula has been drifting slowly westward away from mainland Mexico for the last 20 million years. Espiritu Santo, like most of the islands in the Sea of Cortes is part of the debris left behind by this process. Evidence of the island's former connection to the peninsula is provided by a jagged western shore.

**173. San Lazaro Mountains at the tip of Isla Magdalena.**
Isla Magdalena, only a few miles wide but 55 miles long, serves as a breakwater for the broad expanse of Magdalena Bay. The high level of salinity in the bay waters make it an ideal breeding area for gray whales; the calves cannot help but float to the surface at the moment of their birth, to take their first breath of air.

**174. Early morning fishing launches, Cabo San Lucas.**

**175. Land's end at Cabo San Lucas.**
Government agencies have designated the 20 mile stretch between Cabo San Lucas and San Jose del Cabo as one of five major tourism centers to be developed along the Mexican coast. According to the Los Cabos master plan, the new marina, visible in the background, will one day be surrounded by an air-conditioned emporium of hotels and shopping malls.

**176. An isolated farmstead on the northern Pacific coast of Baja California.**
No other region in Mexico has a population density as low as that of Baja California. Even counting the population of Tijuana, there are only 30 inhabitants per square mile, as opposed to the nationwide average of 107. In fact, isolation is one of the most salient features of life on the peninsula and basic survival is at times the only objective for those who live in the desert.

**177. Isla San Francisquito in the Sea of Cortes.**
The Sea of Cortes is dotted with hundreds of islands, many of which are home to endemic animal species particular to this area, such as the rattleless rattlesnake of Isla Santa Catarina and the spiny-tailed iguanas of Isla San Esteban. The ecology of these islands is finely balanced, so that any sudden changes in the local environment might provoke a chain reaction that would seriously endanger the survival of unique wildlife.

**178/179. Winter plowing by the Pacific, Santo Tomas.**
The northwestern coast of Baja California is the only place in Mexico where a Mediterranean-type climate may be found, with the rainy season in winter rather than in summer. Thick mists moisten the coastline soils, making the area particularly suitable for growing crops, especially tomatoes. Vineyards cover the drier hinterland valleys.

**180. Wind-shaped sand dunes by Scammon's Lagoon.**
Every year between November and March, the grey whales arrive at this and other sites along the Baja California coast to breed. That the lagoon should be known by the name of one of the most notorious whalers of the nineteenth century is an irony mercifully lost on the whales.

**181a. Evaporation patterns on the surface of the salt marshes by Vizcaino Bay.**
Vizcaino Bay, named after one of California's first Spanish explorers, constitutes one of the most starkly beautiful landscapes in the world. It is also a landscape in constant flux. Acres of white salt residues are left when the sea water evaporates after the flats are flooded at high tide. Beneath the relentless sun, the gray-green ponds can disappear within a few days.

**181b. Tractors scoop up salt deposits in Guerrero Negro.**
Here, man has imitated nature's method of extracting salt from the sea. 5,000-acre ponds only a foot-and-a-half deep are periodically flooded and the water left to evaporate. Enormous tractors, with wheels ten feet in diameter, merely have to scrape the crystals from the ground. There are thirty of these ponds, producing annually a hundred thousand tons of salt, most of which are shipped to Japan.

**182. Water flow patterns in the marshes of Guerrero Negro.**

**183. The delta of the Colorado River.**
Before dams and irrigation drastically restricted the volume of water in the Colorado River, the tidal bore of San Felipe was much feared by seamen navigating the Sea of Cortes. After the spring thaw, the swollen Colorado River joined high tides funneled by the narrowing straits of the gulf to produce the treacherous bore. A stationary wave would form, grow within minutes to a height of six or seven feet, and roll violently back inland.

**184/185. Sunset over Concepcion Bay.**